W9-BWD-081

WITHDRAWN

BASKETBALL'S
AMOEBA
DEFENSE

BASKETBALL'S AMOEBA DEFENSE
A COMPLETE MULTIPLE SYSTEM

FRAN WEBSTER

Parker Publishing Company, Inc.
West Nyack, New York

Library of Congress Cataloging in Publication Data

Webster, Fran.
  Basketball's amoeba defense.

  Includes index.
  1. Basketball—Defense. 2. Basketball—Coaching.
3. Basketball—United States—Defense—History.
4. Basketball—United States—Offense—History. I. Title.
GV888.W43 1984   796.32'32   83-23654
ISBN 0-13-069139-9

Printed in the United States of America

DEDICATION

To my lovely wife Ruth, and to our sons Gary and Jim, and our daughters Debra and Leslie, for their everlasting, faithful support in all my endeavors.

ACKNOWLEDGMENTS

My career as a basketball player, official, and coach was an exciting and rewarding experience. This was due to the many good and interesting people I first played with and later worked with along the way. However, a special thanks must be given to John Gazetos, my first coach, now an attorney at law in Butler, Pa., and Coach Buzz Ridl, now athletic director at Westminster College (Pa.). These two men were most responsible for the way my coaching career developed, and thus helped make the writing of this book possible.

I would also like to thank Gary Webster, Mary Jane Krammer, and Louise Gilkey for their assistance in the preparation of this manuscript.

HOW THE AMOEBA DEFENSE
WILL HELP YOU

Pitt's defense is just like an Amoeba. It's constantly changing.

Coach Carl Sloan,
George Washington University, 1974

The experiment with multiple defenses began while I was coaching at the high school level in the late 1950s. The possibility of developing a sophisticated multiple defense became apparent in 1964 at Westminster College and led to the implementation of the technique known today as the jump-switch. This play, the jump-switch, proved to be the central skill in the development of a practical multiple defense system. Ten years later the system became widely known as the Amoeba defense, when the University of Pittsburgh attained national recognition for its successful defense. Since 1975 the number of coaches using the multiple defense has increased, and many believe it will be the defense of the future.

A multiple defense continually shifts from zone to man-to-man and back again. The best multiple defensive systems create confusion, leading to the disruption of even the best offensive units. This book covers every phase of the Amoeba defense—a multiple defensive system which has proved its practical value time after time on the floor. In addition, it will explain (with diagrams) the many ways the Amoeba defense is able to adjust and adapt to any offensive change. *Moreover, it will illustrate precisely where conventional defenses break down against modern offensive systems, and why a multiple defense such as the Amoeba can shore up those breakdowns.*

In 1975 the pamphlet on the Amoeba defense was hastily written to meet an increasing demand for information on the system. In the rush to answer the requests of coaches who were interested in the Amoeba defense. a lot was left unsaid about this system, a system that had taken ten years to develop. This new edition not only covers the Amoeba defense more fully, but adds new material, new drills, and two new sections illustrating many offensive plays which can regularly beat conventional defenses.

The material in the book can be used by coaches of both men's and women's basketball teams. The drills contained in this book stress offensive as well as defensive fundamentals. They can be used by virtually any coach at any level.

In addition to the practical skills, plays, and coaching methods explained in the book, there are three general benefits that need emphasis:

(1) *The Amoeba defense is fun to play.* As most coaches know, it is the rare player who has a natural enthusiasm for playing defense. Most players consider offense the fun side of the game. Defense demands work. This psychological problem adds to the burdens of defensive instruction. But the Amoeba defense is an active, aggressive system. It provides defensive players with a variety of options during a game. A skilled defensive player can take more chances in attempting to create a turnover. He remains confident that he will be backed up by his teammates. The plays and drills in this book are designed with an eye to creating this confidence in a well-trained defensive player. In a game, defensive play has many variables and is more fun.

(2) *The Amoeba defense attacks modern offensive players where they are most vulnerable—the passing game.* Most modern players develop great skills for shooting and moving the ball by dribbling. Their skills at moving the ball by passing are much less well developed. The Amoeba defense, geared to stopping

the dribble and forcing the pass, attacks the modern offense at its weakest link. . . the pass.

(3) *The book provides some insight into the historical development of multiple defenses.* It will help coaches see through historical perspective why multiple defenses will become common over the next few years. The arrival of multiple defense systems is a significant change, allowing progressive coaches to teach the best techniques against today's ever-improving offensive players. Throughout basketball history, as offensive skills improved, the defense was forced to find new ways to stop them. Multiple defense is the most recent attempt and is a requisite of the foreseeable future.

This book is one of the first attempts to publish a comprehensive look at a multiple defense. To my knowledge, there is no other book that covers a multiple defense system with the detail presented here. Each chapter deals with a specific element of the Amoeba defense. I have also tried to put the elements together, providing a look at the seamless, interwoven combination of zone and man-to-man principles that makes up the Amoeba defense.

After publication of the pamphlet in 1975, many coaches expressed disappointment because no discussion of the *keys* that are important to the smooth running of the Amoeba defense was included. A section on *keys* has been inserted into this edition.

Coaches who take the time to master the Amoeba defense system, and to teach it to their players, will send to the floor a defense that will cause even the most effective offensive teams many problems.

Fran Webster

CONTENTS

PART III: TEACHING, SPECIAL DRILLS AND RULES

INTRODUCTORY CHART

Please examine this floor chart before reading the text. In each chapter, frequent references are made to the areas indicated by the names shown.

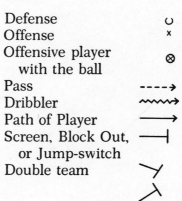

KEY

Defense	ᴗ
Offense	×
Offensive player with the ball	⊗
Pass	----→
Dribbler	∿∿→
Path of Player	⟶
Screen, Block Out, or Jump-switch	—⊣
Double team	⅄

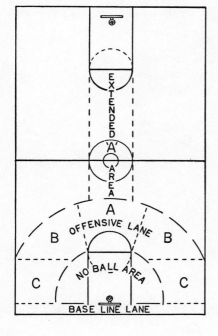

NOTE: A minimum of symbols will be used in each diagram, whenever possible. Sometimes numbers will be used in place of the player symbols, for reasons made clear in the text. The open end of the defensive player symbol ᴗ indicates the position of the defensive player's feet.

17

PART 1:
OFFENSES USED
AGAINST CONVENTIONAL
DEFENSES

1

History of Offense vs Defense, 1925-Present

EARLY SKILLS

Whoever first said "Necessity is the mother of invention" could have been making reference to the way Dr. Naismith first began to play a game called basketball in his physical education classes at Springfield College in 1892. That is exactly why he came up with this new game. He needed more indoor activities for his winter program. Since that day there has been a gradual changing of the rules with the prime purpose of making basketball a more exciting and popular game. This has been accomplished. Basketball, the American game, has more player participation than any other sport in the United States. It has also become a popular sport in almost every nation of the world.

In the United States it was at first a game to play between baseball and football season. Now it is a major sport in most every high school and college in the nation. The offensive skills of the players have improved vastly over the years. This, along with improving coaching techniques in team offense, has put a heavy burden on the defensive phase of the game. Out of *necessity* the defenses have had to be changed in one way or another to counteract the ever-improving offense.

Compared to today's standards, the early offensive skills of the players were crude. Shooting, ball handling, and dribbling efforts were inept. The three skills that most players executed best at this time were the lay-up, passing, and the underhand, two-handed foul shot. Team play began to improve as practice sessions became a regular part of the season. Since the lay-up

21

and other short-range shots were the only good percentage shots for most players, it was necessary to execute the pass well. Excessive dribbling was discouraged. It took away from the team play. Almost everyone used a two-handed underhand foul shot that started from around the waistline or lower. It may seem surprising today that many players attempted this technique in shooting field goal attempts, although the shooter had to be eight or ten feet away from the player guarding him to get the shot off. Some players, especially the offensive guards, started to develop an accurate outside two-handed set shot that started from the chest or eye level. The big players (inside men) began to develop a hook shot from four to ten feet. Thirty points for the winning team was considered a high scoring game.

As in any team sport, there is a constant battle between the offense and defense. To score, the offense tries to finesse the defense into making a mistake. As the offensive skills and coaching improved, the defense was forced to find new ways to stop them. The defense dominated the game until the middle of the 1920s. A good, straight man-to-man defense set up within the offensive lane made it difficult for the offense to penetrate. Limited skill in shooting, passing, and dribbling kept most of the game scores low. Each defensive player's responsibility was to keep his man from scoring. He received only token help from his teammates. It was truly a man-to-man (one-on-one) defense.

ORGANIZED OFFENSE

Straight man-to-man defense soon began to lose its effectiveness when coaches started to organize the team offense through a series of screens and planned plays.

Since outside shooting and dribbling were discouraged, passing was the one skill necessary to get the desired lay-up. Passing was considered the most important offensive skill for a player to have in those early days. The rules committee in the 1920s considered making the dribble illegal. Even the New York Celtics, World Professional Champions at the time, endorsed the action. The Celtics felt that the dribble was a poor substitute for the pass and hurt the game. Regardless of this general feeling, the pass to get the close-in shot did become less important as the players gradually began to improve their shooting and dribbling skills. This, in my opinion, had an adverse effect on the pass. To a degree, the skill for a good sharp penetrating pass became a lost art. The shooting and dribbling skills have improved greatly over these past 50 years. Passing has not gone through such improvements. That deficiency has a lot to do with the type of defense played today. This weakness in today's offensive player was partly instrumental in the development of the Amoeba defense.

FIRST MOTION OFFENSES

It may be a surprise to many coaches, especially the younger ones, that the popular passing or motion offense that many teams are using today was first used in the 1920s. It was used then for the very same reason it is used today. It was able to get the good percentage shot against a tough man-to-man defense. Back in the 1920s the only good percentage shot was the lay-up.

Dr. H. C. Carlson, coach of the University of Pittsburgh (1924–1951) was one of the pioneers in using this type of offense. His offense was spread out more than the one used today. He had a good reason, as will be explained later. Carlson used the same 1-2-2 set, but the players set up in the offensive lane, as shown in *Diagram 2-1*. Today teams usually set up with four players located in the no-ball area as shown in *Diagram* 2-27.

Carlson's offense had most of the screens taking place in the *offensive lane,* enabling the player who cut off the screens to move into the *no-ball area.* (See Introductory Chart on page 17.) If the screen was successful, he could get the uncontested lay-up. Because the weak-side defense help was not perfected during this period, when the defensive man could not fight over a screen, his man would be open for the easy shot. The defensive man was taught to concentrate on his own man. Today, a good man-to-man defense will sag on the weak side and always be ready to help protect the no-ball area. If the defense attempted to use a switching type of man-to-man, the offense with its constant motion and screening would eventually create a mix-up and without the weak-side help, a player would be open for the moving lay-up.

This was an ideal offense for the period. Good outside shooters were rare. Even the best college teams only had one good outside shooter, two at the most. A good field goal percentage for a team was around 35 percent. When Carlson was having his greatest success with this offense, he allowed only one player (his best shooter) to shoot beyond 12 ft. He believed in a ball-control offense. He would have his team pass the ball, no matter how long it took, until they got the high percentage shot. It must be remembered that the preventive or closed stance type of guarding (one pass away) was not taught at this time. A player was instructed to stay between his man and the basket at all times. Today, this would be called a passive defense.

Dr. Carlson was so successful with this offense that he won two mythical national championships during the late 1920s. They did not have a national play-off back then. Playing a schedule that took in much of the United States, his teams were undefeated in 1927–28 and won 23 games while losing two in 1929–30. Dr. Carlson was able to win 80 percent of his games for a twelve year period from 1926 to 1937. He was one of the first coaches inducted into the *Naismith Basketball Hall of Fame.*

ZONE DEFENSE THE ANSWER

It was Carlson and coaches who used a similar man-to-man offense who were partly responsible for making the various zone defenses popular in the mid-thirties and into the forties and fifties. It is interesting to note that after most teams began to play a zone defense against his teams, Carlson was able to maintain only a 50 percent winning record for the remaining years that he coached. Although there were other factors behind this decline, having to play against the zone was one of the most important.

Yes, the various zones were the answer in forcing teams out of this type of offense. The zone enabled the defense to close off the passing lanes in the no-ball area. It was more difficult to get the lay-up as screening-type zone offenses were rarely used at this time. Now, the majority of shots had to be taken from 10 feet or beyond. Usually this shot would be from a stand-still or set position. The tight zone (four defensive players always within the no-ball area) forced the offense to shoot more outside shots. Good outside shooting would pull the defense out, easing the offense's task of penetrating for closer shots. The zone now made it necessary for coaches to encourage the players to work on improving their outside shooting skills.

RULE CHANGES FAVOR OFFENSE

The history of team sports in America clearly shows that when rules are changed, it usually favors the offense. There is good reason for this and it should not be unduly criticised. The spectators enjoy successful offensive play more than they enjoy defense. It is more exciting to the average spectator when the offenses of two teams dominate the game. Also, most players enjoy playing on the offense more than the defense. This is especially true in basketball. It cannot be denied that the popularity of the game has increased in direct proportion to the increase in higher scoring games. The rules committee did its part in 1932 with the ten second rule and again in 1937 by taking the center jump after each score out of the game. With the ball being taken out at the end court after each score, a new offensive threat appeared—*the fast break*—creating more action and a much faster game. The rule change made it possible for more fast break situations and gave the offense more opportunity to get the ball in good scoring position before the defense could set up and protect the no-ball area. Now it was possible to score from 30 to 60 percent of the team's points on a quick transition or fast break.

ONE-HAND SET AND JUMP SHOT

But perhaps more significant than the rule change in strengthening the offense was the advent of two new offensive fundamentals. These offensive threats were the *one-hand set* and the *jump shot*. Until this time, the only outside stand-still shot was the two-hand set, not a good percentage shot for most players. The one-hand set came on the scene in the early 1940s. Coaches and players soon discovered that the one-hand set was not only more accurate, but could be released much quicker. Just a few years later, players started to use a one-hand jumpshot which proved to be even more accurate from the 10- to 20-foot distance. It was much more effective and accurate than the "hook" shot from the 4- to 12-foot distance, and much easier to get off in close quarters than the one-hand set shot.

Many players from the high school level and up had, by the 1950s, become proficient with these shots. The improved outside shooting now took away much of the advantage of a tight zone defense. The accuracy with the outside shot forced the tight defense to move out. The dribble had also become a much more effective offensive weapon. Gradually, many players were becoming very skillful with the dribble and could easily *outmaneuver* a defensive player in a one-and-one situation. This gave the offense another way to penetrate the no-ball area for the good percentage shot or pass off after penetration to a teammate for the same type of shot.

DEFENSE CHANGE

Coaches who were disciples of man-to-man defense began to apply more pressure on the ball and instructed the weak-side defense to sag toward the no-ball area along with the *help and recovery* defensive tactic. This sagging defense closed off the passing and dribbling lanes, slowing up the effectiveness of the offense. Coaches oriented to the man-to-man would use a zone defense only as a last resort or for a change of pace. There were still many coaches, however, who preferred the zone defense, using it as the primary defense, only resorting to man-to-man when the zone failed. A new type of zone defense also appeared in the fifties, called the "match-up" defense. It was very difficult to teach, but was successful in slowing the offense when executed properly. This defense attempts to have each player protect a certain area "matching up" with the various offensive sets. Each player would use a combination of zone and man-to-man defensive principles in guarding the offensive player in his area.

Varicus man and zone presses were also used during the fifties. Until this time, pressure defenses were usually only used in the late stages of a game when the losing team tried to change the course of the game. In the fifties, teams started using pressure defenses at any stage of the game. The defense was becoming much more aggressive.

All these various defenses were used in an attempt to stop the ever-improving offense. At that time, coaches believed that a player had to shoot at least over 40 percent from the field or he would be hurting the offense. Team averages were ranging from 42 to 50 percent from the field.

The popularity of basketball began to increase considerably in all areas of the United States after World War II. It had more player participation than any other sport. Basketball was becoming a great spectator sport and larger arenas were being built to accommodate the increase.

LEADERS IN WESTERN PENNSYLVANIA

There were several coaches who were most responsible for the type of basketball that was played in Western Pennsylvania in this half century (1925–1980). They also had a great deal of influence on my development as a basketball coach. In the early years they were Dr. Carlson, University of Pittsburgh; Chic Davies, Duquesne University; Dr. John Lawther, Westminister and Penn State; and Pappy Washabaugh, Westminster. Each made a specific contribution: Dr. Carlson, with his motion offense; Davies, with his offensive and defensive tactics; Lawther with his 3-2 and 2-3 zone defenses; and Washabaugh, with his full court man-to-man pressure. Later there were Buzz Ridl, Westminister, with his deliberate offense; Edward McCluskey, Farrell High School, with his "hard nose" and pressing man-to-man defense; and Butler Hennon, Wampum High School, with his high scoring offense using the fastbreak and one-hand set shots. They were the leaders that other coaches looked to in determining the type of offense or defense to use. The reader who does not live in or near Western Pennsylvania may not know anything about the coaches named; but certainly there were coaches that had this same kind of influence on the manner in which basketball was taught in all the different geographical areas.

NATIONAL MAJOR SPORT

Up to the 1940s, geographical areas were isolated from one another, each tending to develop its own particular style of play. This began to gradually change in 1937; Dr. Carlson held the first basketball clinic and invited coaches from all over the country. The National Basketball Association of Coaches was formed in the same year. The beginning of the national NCAA basketball tournament to determine a national championship began in 1939. More universities began to play schedules taking them to all parts of the United States. Colleges in the Southeast and other areas of the United States where basketball had just started to gain popularity began to recruit high school players from other sections of the nation, where there was a greater abundance of talented players. World War II (1941–45) played a part in spreading the popularity of the game in these areas. Basketball was a game that the military leaders encouraged soldiers to play in their spare time during the training period. Every camp had a number of inside and outside basketball courts. Many of these camps were located in areas where basketball had been slow in developing. Basketball had finally become a national sport like football and baseball. The media, book and magazine publications, clinics, television, and large basketball arenas assisted in making the game a popular spectator sport.

Talented athletes began to play basketball the year 'round to improve their skills. Black athletes were finally given the opportunity to show their skills in the game. They soon proved that they had the ability to adapt to the skills necessary in the modern game of basketball. This ability became a dominant force in improving all aspects of the skills necessary to make the game a more attractive spectator sport.

Professional basketball, which until this time had never had much to offer in the way of financial benefits, began to get the necessary backing to form a league where top players could earn a good salary. Out of all this the professional National Basketball Association (NBA) was formed.

MY FIRST MULTIPLE DEFENSE

When I started my first high school coaching job in 1947, the one-hand set was being used by most of the high school players, and many were beginning to perfect the one-hand jump-shot. By the 1950s, the skills of the offensive player had improved so much with these two shots, some teams began to average over 80 points a game and sometimes would go over the hundred mark. The offense was definitely dominating the game. Before these two shots were used a good defensive man could give an excellent offensive player a difficult time on a one-on-one situation. *Now, an excellent defensive player would have trouble stopping an average offensive player playing one-on-one.* Players had also improved their dribbling skill greatly, adding to the defense's woes.

I had fair success in my first ten years as a coach, but never was happy with the way my teams played defense. Depending on the type of players I had, my primary defense would be man-to-man mixed with some zone or vice-versa. This led in the late fifties to experimenting with a combination defense. The defenses used each time the opponents had the ball were determined by *keys*. For example, the defense played sometimes was determined by where the opponents put the ball in play from out-of-bounds. Many other keys were also used, and finally a defense was found that helped win games. This multiple defense was the most important factor in making it possible for my team, Hickory Township, to reach the Pennsylvania State Finals in Class AAA in 1961.

BIRTH OF AMOEBA

In 1962, I accepted a position at Westminster College (PA.) as a Physical Education instructor and Assistant Basketball Coach. Westminster was noted for its fine basketball teams. Buzz Ridl was the head coach. His teams were in the NAIA play-offs practically every year. In 1964–65 we lost in the district finals by one point and failed to get to the tournament in Kansas City. The team had shot an amazing 62 percent from the field and still lost. Shortly after, in a discussion about the next year's plans, Buzz said, "We have to do something about our defense. It's crazy to lose a game when your team shoots 62 percent." The next year the experimentation with a multiple defense system began. This led to the development of the Amoeba defense.

The basic premise of the Amoeba defense is to disrupt the pass, the weakest link in the modern player's offensive fundamentals. The skilled players today can all shoot the jump shot with great accuracy from a distance of approximately 21 ft. Most have great dribbling skills. Few have great passing skills, and many are poor in executing this offensive fundamental. When pressure is applied on the ball by using a full, three-quarter, or half court press, many players can be forced into throwing erratic passes. A pressure defense may produce the same poorly executed pass even after the offense has been able to set up their planned offense in the offensive lane. Because of the great shooting talent of the players today, creating a *turnover* is the most productive play the defense can make. The Amoeba defense, by applying pressure on the ball in all its various defensive alignments, is attempting to create this *turnover*.

This multiple defense helped Westminster win 20 games or more the next three years (1966 through 1968). Buzz was hired as head basketball coach at the University of Pittsburgh in 1968. I followed the next year as assistant coach in charge of defense. The Amoeba was an important factor in carrying Pitt to the Eastern Finals of the NCAA tournament in 1974 and to the NIT in 1975.

MULTIPLE DEFENSE TODAY

There are many teams now using the multiple defense in one way or another. Coaches are finding that this is one way to slow up the constantly improving offensive systems used today. As the zone defense was the answer to slowing up Carlson's motion offense in the 1930s, the multiple defense is the answer to slowing it up in the 1980s.

Carlson's motion offense, with most of the screens in the offensive lane, was successful because it could produce the easy lay-up. Today's motion offense, by setting up most of its screens in the no-ball area, will produce the 10- to 18-foot jump shot that most players shoot well today. The zone defense can force teams out of this offense, but it is vulnerable to the outside one-hand set or jump shot. Today, there are also good screening and penetrating type offenses that can render a zone defense helpless. Coaches are finding by combining pressure (half-court, three-quarter court, and full court) defense, and changing from man-to-man to zone and back again frequently during the course of the game, the offense can be kept off balance, shooting accuracy can be reduced, and patterns disrupted. This is exactly what the Amoeba defense does.

The Amoeba defense system was one of the first multiple defenses, and it still might be the most sophisticated. When executed properly, it is difficult for the offense to determine what defense is being employed as they move to the front court to set up their offense. The Amoeba constantly interweaves man-to-man principles with zone principles. Certain *keys* determine the way in which these principles will interweave. The Amoeba is a combination of most of the defenses that have been used up to this time, plus a few relatively new defensive fundamentals.

The offense, with the constant improvement of individual fundamentals and coordinated team play, has forced coaches to experiment with multiple defenses. Even the most ardent man-to-man defensive coach will have to grudgingly admit that the most effective man-to-man defenses today are using zone principle practically everywhere on the floor except on the ball. The same can be said about the coaches who prefer the zone. The best zones are of the match-up variety; they are constantly adjusting and use man-to-man principles in the area they are defending. The double team which was used mostly in zone defenses has recently become a very important maneuver in many man-to-man defenses. The pro teams in the NBA that are not allowed to use zone defenses as such, are using various zone principles in all areas except on the ball. It is interesting to note a statement made by a professional coach after his team had two technical fouls called against it for playing zone defense in a game played March 1, 1981. He said, "It's *our* defense, it's not *zone* defense. You could make the same call on each NBA ball club a dozen times each game."

Recently another offense has been giving the defense a real problem. The slow-up four corner offense is frustrating the best-laid plans of many defenses. This offense has been around for years, but it was seldom used until the last few minutes of the game to protect a narrow lead; or, when playing a team that was far superior, the underdog tried to keep the score down. Today, teams (even favored teams) that get an early lead may go into this type of stall during the last five or so minutes of the *first half*. Many teams now employ this stall early in the second half when they have a substantial lead. This is especially true when the team in the lead has key men in foul trouble or is playing away from home. It can be very frustrating for the team that is behind. A team in a four-corner spread slow-up will only attempt a field goal when it has the highest percentage shot. The defense must go after it. If the offense executes well, it usually forces the defense to foul or eventually gets the easy shot. There are several defense strategies I consider best to force a four-corner offense into turnovers and out of this offense. These will be dealt with in a later chapter.

A defense that has gained popularity again in recent years is the passive 2-3 zone. Some of the top college teams in the country are even making this their primary defense. The main reason for this is the difficulty coaches have in getting big, talented offensive players to play good man-to-man against the tough motion and passing offenses. It is easier to have three big men lay back, protecting the no-ball area. This forces the offense to shoot from outside. When the shot is missed, the offensive rebound is more difficult. The 2-3 is one of the better defensive rebounding defenses. The 2-3 is also less tiring than any other defense. Now, the talented offensive players are able to save energy for the offensive. They will only come out of the 2-3 when they get behind and need to play aggressive defense to win the game. There are also other reasons for many teams resorting to this defense. The 2-3 accomplishes the same thing for the defense as the four-corner does for the offense. After gaining a substantial lead by using a more aggressive defense, the team now can set back in the 2-3 and force its opponents to make the outside shot to get back into the game. Often, when a team is forced to score from outside, players tighten up and have trouble making even the good percentage outside shot. As mentioned, this defense doesn't give up many second shots. The passive 2-3 is also used for a few minutes at various times to give a hard working, aggressive defense a rest. Teams that lack overall team speed and have two or three 6'8" to 6'11" players will also resort to this defense in an attempt to give the opponent only the outside shot, while still reducing offensive rebound chances.

The change-of-pace type of basketball that has emerged in the late seventies in both offensive and defensive strategies has made the game scores range from the low forties up to a hundred or more. If the deliberate offense and passive defense dominate the game, the scores are low. If the fast transition (fastbreak) offense and pressing defense dominate, the scores are high. If the games are mixed with a little of both, the scores are in the medium range. The 1980s will continue to produce this kind of basketball with the continual improvement of the offense, along with the gradual development of the multiple defense to counteract it.

✳ SUMMARY ✳

Basketball, especially in high school and colleges has become a game of strategy. It is now an exciting game of "cat and mouse." Coaches are constantly adjusting their offense or defense to get that one step ahead necessary to assure victory. This chapter has given a brief view of the manner in which the gradually improving offense in basketball over the past half century has determined the development of various defenses, keeping a respectable balance with the offense. Quality offense is what has made the game of basketball a popular sport. The rules of the game make it possible for the offense to have a slight edge on the defense. This is the way it should be. However, the defense cannot afford to let the offense get too far ahead, or the game could lose some of its popularity. This, I believe, is happening in the NBA. The players are so adept in their offensive skills that the defense seems helpless in too many games. Lately the attendance has fallen off at pro games. The knowledgeable fan wants to see more than a shooting contest. Although the name of the game is scoring, the defense must constantly be finding ways to keep the offense in check.

The multiple defense system is an effort to counter the improved skills of today's offensive player. These individual skills plus the ever-improving coaching technique in team offense has placed the conventional defenses at a great disadvantage in trying to prevent the good percentage shot. The regular man-to-man, zones and match-up defenses used today are usually only effective when the team is so *superior* that it makes no difference what kind of defense is used. Even the "hardnose" man-to-man defense that some coaches employ is only successful when the officials hesitate to call defensive fouls that occur. When the defense fights through legal screens, uses body and arms to jam up the center, or pushes offensive players out of the offensive lanes through brute strength, illegal defensive tactics usually take place.

What must you do to have an effective defense today? You must have a defense that is able to finesse the offense. You must use defensive tactics that will keep the offense out of its team patterns. You must have a flexible defense that is able to adjust to every offensive change an opponent may make. You must provoke the offense into doing what you want it to do.

No defense can be effective today if it allows the offense to get into a planned attack. *Pressure must be kept on the ball* as much as possible during the entire game. With most teams shooting from *45 to 60* percent from the field today, the biggest play in the game is *recovery*. Every time the defense forces an opponent into a *turnover* it results in a 1.5 to 4 point advantage for the team that causes the turnover. The multiple defense or "Amoeba" has averaged over 20 recoveries per game each year from 1965 to 1980. When the offense is finessed, turnovers are created.

There are many offensive systems that are very successful against the conventional defenses. These same offensive systems have difficulty playing against a good multiple defense. This is especially true if various methods of concealing the defense are used until the ball enters the front court offensive lane area. The "Amoeba" defense is noted for this characteristic. It may even change from zone to man or vice versa after the ball enters the offensive lane.

The next two chapters show you a number of offenses that have been successful against the conventional defenses. Then in the following chapters the "Amoeba" defense will be presented. It will demonstrate why the offenses that have been very successful against the conventional defenses have much more difficulty in being as effective against a multiple defense like the "Amoeba."

2

Man-to-Man Offenses

EARLY MOTION OFFENSES

This chapter presents the three stages of the eventual development of the modern motion or passing man-to-man offense. The first stage began in the 1920s, led by the World Champion New York Celtics and eventually college coaches. The second stage was developed in the 1950s, led by Coach Joel Evans of Auburn and his famous "Shuffle Offense." Other systems branched off of this, like the offense I used during this same period, which is illustrated in detail in this chapter. During the 1970s, the modern motion or "passing" offense developed gradually from the "Stack" offense. It is without question the most popular man-to-man offense in basketball today.

The New York Celtics made famous a wheel-like offense with the pivot as the spoke in the center in the 1920s. The pivot man was allowed to station himself in the foul lane area at the time, because there was no three-second violation. The other four players would pass the ball around and then into the pivot creating a variety of "give-and-go" plays as they cut toward the basket after their pass. They relied more on their clever passing and cutting than on the screen to get open for the good close-in shot.

Later in the 1920s, Dr. Carlson used a 1-2-2 set, with all five players stationed in the offensive lane, leaving the foul lane area open for the players to cut off a screen into this open area for a pass to get the lay-up.

These offenses and others like them were mostly responsible for the development of the various zones and team type man-to-man defenses that are in evidence today. Following are several of these offenses with illustrations.

FIGURE EIGHT—MOTION AND PASSING OFFENSE IN THE OFFENSIVE LANE

Dr. Carlson, in his book *You and Basketball*, wrote on page 77, "The offense is the highlight in any sport. The common saying that 'a good offense is the best defense' holds true in basketball because to keep possession of the ball is to keep on the offensive and eliminate any scoring opportunities for the opposition." He certainly proved that to be true in the 1920s with his continuity passing offense. The man-to-man defense of the time, with its almost total concentration on the player each man was assigned to guard, could not satisfactorily stop his offense. *Almost all the screens in this offense took place in the offensive lane.* It was designed to keep the cutting lanes through the no-ball area to the basket open, eventually leading to the desired lay-up.

The offense he used was based on two fundamental offensive moves, the pass and go around, which he called "Over and Around," and the man-ahead-of-the-ball offense, which he called the "Revolution." Later, a part of this offense became known as Dr. Carlson's Figure Eight. Under certain circumstances, this offense can still be effective today. It makes a good second offense to have when your primary offense is not doing well. It is not difficult for the players to learn and is also a very good offense to use in practice; it can teach your players the proper footwork in guarding an offensive player cutting toward the basket from the offensive lane.

I used the "figure eight" in high school with success in the fifties against teams that played a tight and aggressive man defense on the weak-side offensive players. I also employed it as a slow-up or stall offense. We used this offense at both Westminster and Pitt for the same reasons.

Diagrams 2-1 through *2-5* show the figure eight offense through one complete cycle of its continuity. It starts from a 3-2

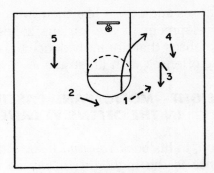

Diagram 2-1

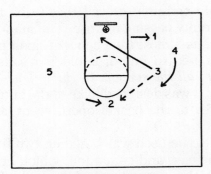

Diagram 2-2

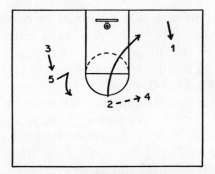

Diagram 2-3

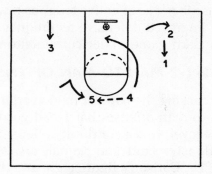

Diagram 2-4

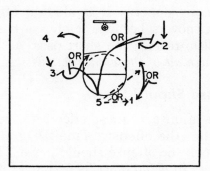

Diagram 2-5

set, 1 passes to 3 and cuts toward basket, etc. for a complete cycle.

To keep proper balance, the passer after his cut will move to the ball side of court. The first option in this is a pass to the cutter moving toward the basket after his pass. This is the old "give-and-go" play, as shown in *Diagram 2-1,* where 3 passes to 1. There are many other options that may be used within the continuity. *Diagram 2-5* shows a few of them. Player 1's man is overplaying him, so 1 goes back door. Player 5 passes to 1 as he moves toward the basket. The diagram also shows 5 passing to 1, and then screening for 3 or 2. It also shows him maintaining continuity.

This offense is not as effective today as it was fifty years ago because of the improved defensive techniques, but it still has a place in the modern game under certain situations.

2-1-2 MAN-TO-MAN OFFENSE

Before discussing the popular motion offense, I am going to explain a man-to-man offense that I had good success with at the high school level. It is a continuity offense that sets screens in both the offensive land and no-ball area. In a way it is a combination of Dr. Carlson's figure eight and the motion offense used today. It has constant motion from a 2-1-2 set with good floor balance at all times. It is difficult for the most aggressive man defense to push this offense out of the offensive lane because of its many options. It is also an offense that has a minimum of turnovers because it always has a man moving toward the ball to receive the short pass. *A successful motion offense must have all of these characteristics.*

Where Offense Should Start

A pattern offense is most effective when you keep the movement within the offensive lane. *Diagram 2-6* shows the area within which the offense should move. *The initial pass or dribble may begin from outside this perimeter,* but all movement in the pattern until the play is completed should remain inside the offensive lanes. If the defense forces the pattern outside this perimeter, the timing and rhythm is upset and the play will not be nearly as effective.

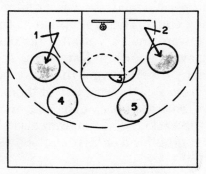

Diagram 2-6

No-Ball Area

Most defenses attempt to keep the ball from entering the area known as the "no-ball area." Offensive men setting up inside this area will usually be fronted by the defensive man. However, to front your man beyond this 15-foot radius is very difficult and dangerous, because of the back door maneuvers of most offenses. Only the quickest and most alert defensive player can front his man successfully beyond the 15-foot radius. Most coaches will have their defensive man loosen up when the offensive player moves beyond this distance.

With this in mind, the offense should try to get the initial pass or screen just outside this 15-foot radius. The ideal spots in this offense are shown in *Diagram 2-6*. The movement of the inside men should try to be no more than 3 feet to 6 feet beyond this 15 feet. The movement of the guards or outside men should be from 3 feet to 6 feet inside the 25-foot radius or offensive lane.

If the defense forces your players beyond this area, then you use your various "back door" options to loosen up the defense.

How the Diagrams Illustrate the Offense

In order to keep from having too many movements on each diagram, only the pass or dribble that keys the play will be illustrated. All the options the player with the ball has will be explained in detail. Also, to give you a clear picture of the continuity of the offense, it will show the new position of each player at completion of play in the next diagram. In other words, the player with the ball will use none of the options, but merely pass the ball back to the guard, so he can begin the next play.

Key to Plays

Key to Play—Dribble by Guard—Diagram 2-7

When 5 starts his dribble toward 2, 2 fakes a move toward the basket and moves out toward the dribbler to set a screen for him. He holds the screen for only a second or two, and then cuts toward the foul line, making a running screen for 3, and continues on to set a screen for 1.

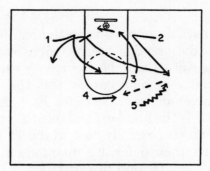

Diagram 2-7

Options 5 has:

1. If 2's screen is effective, 5 may continue his dribble for a jump shot or lay-up.
2. If the defensive men switch, he may pass to 2, who has the option to roll toward basket if he feels he is open.
3. Pass to 3 as he moves toward the basket off the running screen made by 2.
4. Pass to 1 as he moves to the foul line area.
5. If 2 can see that 5 is ahead of his defensive man, he clears out immediately and 5 dribbles in close for lay-up or jump shot. (See *Diagram 2-15* for clear-out play.)

Key—Pass and Follow—Diagram 2-8

When 5 passes back to 4, he immediately moves toward position 2 had on previous play. Player 4 passes ball to 5 and

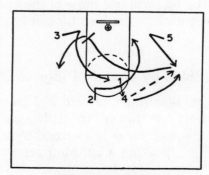

Diagram 2-8

follows, 5 returns ball by pass or hand off. Player 5 then rolls toward the key making a running screen for 2, who is cutting for the basket off a screen set up by 1. Player 5 continues over to weak side and screens for 3, who moves to the high post area.

Options 4 has:

1. Dribbles off 5's screen for a lay-up or jump shot.
2. If defense switches, he could pass to 5, who may roll toward basket.
3. Passes to 2, who, if timing is right, will be cutting off double screen set up by 1 and running screen by 5. Player 1 moves to guard position.
4. Pass to 3 at the high post position.
5. After 5 and 2 have cleared out, 4 may go one-on-one. If 4 passes to 3, he has the option to run the split.

Key to Split—Pass to High Post and Follow—Diagram 2-9

Options 3 has:

1. Fake hand off to 4 and pass to 1 as he cuts to basket. *NOTE:* It is best not to give ball to first cutter on split.
2. Pivot and face basket then pass to 2 for jump shot.
3. Make late pass to 1 under basket.
4. Fake to both 4 and 1 and move to his left for shot, using 1 as screen as he cuts by him.

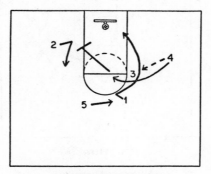

Diagram 2-9

If 4 uses none of these options he passes back to 1. This split can also be initiated by the guard, 1, as in *Diagram 2-10.* 2-1-2 set is ready for next play.

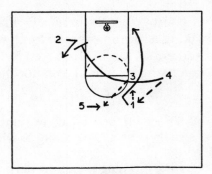

Diagram 2-10

Key—Pass and Go Away from Ball—Diagram 2-11

Player 5 passes to 4 and moves away from ball setting double screen along with 3 for 2. After 2's cut, 1 moves into high post; 3 moves to guard position.

Options 4 has:

1. Passes to 2.
2. Passes to 3 who moves toward ball off of 2 heels for jump shot.
3. Player 4 passes back to 3, who moves out to guard position when he doesn't receive pass for jumper.

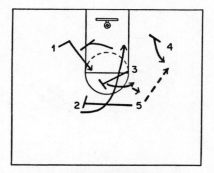

Diagram 2-11

Key—Bounce Pass for Shuffle—Diagram 2-12

The bounce pass from guard to other guard position keys the shuffle play. The famous shuffle has been one of the most effective man-to-man offenses for years. When used in this offensive system, the weak-side guard cutting off the screen often

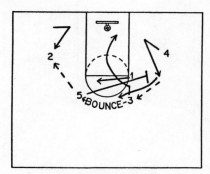

Diagram 2-12

catches the defense by surprise. Player 3 passes to 5, 5 passes to 2, 3 cuts off 1's screen, 5 exchanges positions with 4. Players must be reminded to always be looking for the *bounce pass* between the guards.

Options 2 has:

1. Pass to 3 for lay-up.
2. Pass to 1 for jumper.
3. Pass back to 4 to set up for another play. (*Diagram 2-13*).

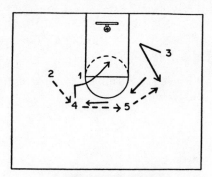

Diagram 2-13

Now 4 has the option of continuing the shuffle or starting a new play. In *Diagram 2-13* he runs the shuffle again. In *Diagram 2-14* he runs the play illustrated in *Diagram 2-7*. You can see by this time how the plays mesh together to make a continuity of motion with a minimum of adjustment after each play.

It was mentioned previously that to get the best results from a patterned offense you must keep the defense from push-

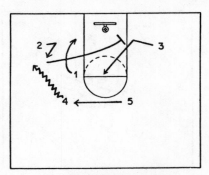

Diagram 2-14

ing you out of the offensive lane. Also, the initial pass should not be beyond twenty feet from the basket.

The only way this can be accomplished against a good pressure type defense is to use the *backdoor* movement effectively. Also a must in any pattern offense is a forward's ability to fake a back door, then move out quickly to receive the pass. It is also important that he vary the fake. It may take only one step or it might take three or four. If the defensive player is still making him move too far out to receive the pass, a combination of the back door and clear-out play will loosen up the over-guarding.

If 2 does not pass to 4 on the back door move, he has three other options (*Diagram 2-15*).

    1. If he has not used his dribble he can go one-on-one against his defensive player.

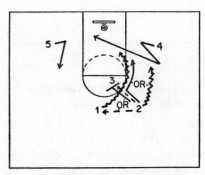

Diagram 2-15

2. Pass to the other guard, fake cut, and set *down* screen for 1 to drive off it.
3. Pass to high post and using a fake, cut toward basket for a "give and go."

The previous diagram illustrated how to loosen up the players guarding the forwards. The next two diagrams will show how to do the same when the guards are overplayed.

In *Diagram 2-16* the defensive player X^1 has been giving 1 a tough time by playing him close and to the strong side, making it difficult for him to follow his pass to 5, so he fakes 1, 2, or 3 steps to the strong side and goes back door.

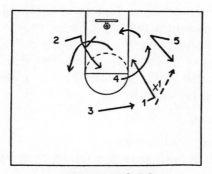

Diagram 2-16

Options for 5 are:

1. Return pass to 1 for "give and go."
2. Pass to 4 cutting off 1's heels.
3. Pass to 2 at high post.
4. Go one-on-one on defensive player.

In *Diagram 2-17,* 5 is unable to use any of these options, so he tries to pass back to 3 but X^2 is overplaying and he is unable to do this. Player 3 does not hesitate and goes back door.

Options 5 has:

1. Pass to 3.
2. Pass back to 2, who takes guard position.

These two moves should take the pressure off the guards and keep the offense moving within the offensive lane. The move 3 makes going back door can be used on any attempted

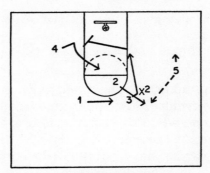

Diagram 2-17

pass back to the guard from the forward. The player at high post will always replace him to keep offense moving.

If the defensive player is playing the dribbler on the strong side, as illustrated in *Diagram 2-18*, the dribbler can change directions and use 4 for screen. Player 1 moves toward the baseline to keep his man busy.

Options for 2 are:

    1. Take jumper off screen.
    2. If switch is made pass to 4 rolling to basket.

This play requires only three players in rotation—2, 4 and 5. If 2 can do neither option, he passes back to 1 or 5 and offense is set for the next play.

NOTE: I have illustrated only the plays moving to offensive right. All these plays may be used going to the left also.

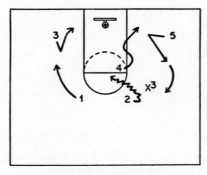

Diagram 2-18

Slow-Up Offense

This continuity offense can also be used effectively if you desire to play a slow-up game against a superior opponent or for other reasons. Using the variety of plays the offense offers and with the constant movement of having a player moving toward the ball on the perimeter (offensive lane), plus the backdoor movements with immediate replacement, you can hold the ball indefinitely with proper execution.

If you are slowing your offense in order to get the last shot of the first half of the game, a play that has worked well through the years is shown in *Diagram 2-19*. With from twelve to fifteen seconds to go, 2 starts the play with a pass to 5 or dribbles toward him—the same keys that are used for plays shown in *Diagrams 2-7* and *2-8*. However, when 5 rolls to make running screen for 4, instead of continuing on and screening for 3, he loops around 4 who is moving toward basket; 2 passes to 5 for a 15-foot jump shot (high percentage shot). Players 3 and 4 get in good position for the rebound if shot is missed, 1 loops away from the lane area to keep his man busy, then follows the shot for the long rebound. This play usually will catch 5's defensive man by surprise. He thinks 5 is moving across to screen for 3, as in the regular plays *(Diagrams 2-7 and 2-8)*. This play was only used in situations like above or as an *out-of-bounds* play in the front court. We would call time out with fifteen seconds to go when playing against man-to-man and use this play starting from out-of-bounds as shown also in *Diagram 2-19*. If 5 beat his man on direct cut to basket 2 would pass to him. This rarely

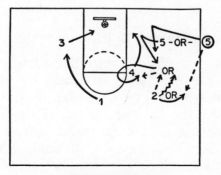

Diagram 2-19

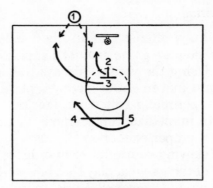

Diagram 2-20

happened, so he would reverse his direction and play would develop as illustrated. We would also use this play during a game, when we had a big lead, just to get practice for a game situation when a field goal was really needed.

Another out-of-bounds play that was very successful against man-to-man when the ball was out-of-bounds underneath the basket is illustrated in *Diagram 2-20*. Most teams today use a zone defense to protect the basket on in-bound plays from this position. However, some diehard man-to-man coaches still play *man*. This play often results in a high percentage shot. Player 1 passes either to 3 for the 8-foot jump shot or to 2 for the lay-up. Player 3 fakes right then goes to his left off of 2's screen. If the defense *switches,* 2 makes a reverse pivot on his right foot which puts him in front of the defensive player now guarding him. On switch 3 has pulled the other defensive man away from the foul lane area; 2 moves in for lay-up. If they do *not* switch 3 often gets an uncontested short jump shot.

Man-to-Man Offensive Drills

The best type of drills on offensive fundamentals at the high school or college level is usually for the fundamentals necessary to execute your type of offense. In the drills that follow, the players will be learning the offense and at the same time be practicing all the important offensive fundamentals such as ball handling, passing, dribbling, shooting, pivoting, faking, screening, offensive rebounding, play without the ball, and all the other essential fundamentals that are necessary to execute a good man-to-man offense.

Diagram 2-21

A two-man drill for this offense is shown in *Diagram 2-21*. Player 1 passes to 2. Player 2 must move to receive the pass with his *right* foot forward. It is best if he receives the ball just before he is completely stopped. Player 2 *hands* the ball back to 1 like a football quarterback, then rolls toward *foul line*, and near the foul line he makes a right angle cut to the basket pushing off on his *left foot* when he changes direction. He must also practice a *change of pace* on this cut. Player 1 returns the pass to him for a *lay-up* or fakes pass and using a *"jab" step* makes a *one-on-one drive* to the basket as 2 clears out. Player 1 takes 2's position, 2 goes to end of line. *NOTE:* In this one elementary drill I can count *nine* offensive fundamentals the players are working on and at the same time learning a part of the team offense.

Diagram 2-22. The split three-man drill may be initiated by either 1 or 2; the passer always cuts first. Player 3 may hand off to second cutter. He may fake hand off and pivot on right or

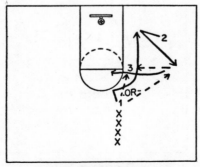

Diagram 2-22

left foot and face the basket. Player 3 then may pass to 1, who sets up in low post area, take the jump shot, or fake the shot and drive for a closer shot. This is just an example of the type of two and three man drills you can use out of this offense; there are many more.

Diagrams 2-23 and 24—Five Man Drill. This five man drill uses two plays from the offense. They must not try to score until they get into the second play. In *Diagram 2-23* they are running the shuffle as was illustrated in *Diagram 2-12*. Player 4 passes back to 2, who immediately goes into play shown in *Diagram 2-24*. Player 2's dribble keys play, 4 makes running screen for 3, who cuts toward basket receiving pass from 2 for lay-up. He may also use other options the play offers. There are many other two-play variations you can use in the five man drill. This type of drill gives the team practice in going from one play to another.

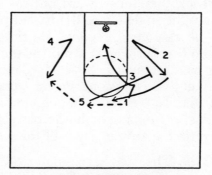

Diagram 2-23

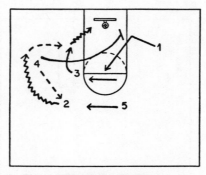

Diagram 2-24

They run through the entire first play but must make some type of scoring attempt on the second play. You may combine any two plays in the offense in this drill. These two-play drills help build the confidence of the players in moving from one play to another. Through repetition the players soon learn what their responsibility is in each offensive position of every play.

Favorite Two-Play Drill

Many coaches do not like to use a continuity offense if it has their center and big forward move out to the guard position. This offense does have them move to the guard position, but not for long. *Diagrams* 2-25 and 26 illustrate how we handled the problem. When we started this offense, we always had our center and big forward set up in the high (1) and low (3) post area as shown in *Diagram* 2-25. The pass and follow play would bring

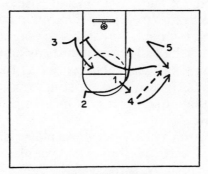

Diagram 2-25

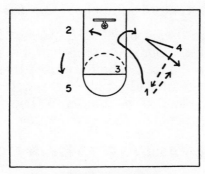

Diagram 2-26

our high post man (1 center) out to the guard position. If 4 did not use any of the options in the first play, he passed back to 1. After passing back, 4 immediately would take two to three steps toward baseline and then move out for return pass from 1. Player 1 (our center) would not run a regular play, but would cut toward the basket on the old "give and go" (*Diagram 26*). If 4 could not pass to him as he cut, 1 would stop in low post and turn toward ball a few steps. If he was able to pin his defensive man behind him 4 would then pass to him. Player 1 would then attempt to use a power move to get a close-in shot. This maneuver kept our big men handling the ball in the backcourt to a minimum and at same time added another effective play to our offense. If 4 did not pass to 1, he dribbles back to guard position and the rest of the offensive players with a minimum of movement would be ready for next play. Anytime we had a player in the guard position we did not want there, he would run this play immediately and get back to an inside position.

This play is in the *two-play drill* section because it makes a great drill for the big men. It teaches the big man exactly what to do when he has the ball in the guard position. He merely uses the old "give and go" play and moves to the inside position where he belongs. It also is surprising how many times he is wide open for a lay-up on this play or gets good inside position for a power move.

We would run the two and three player drills for one week before using defensive players. The two-play drills were practiced for approximately three weeks before using defensive players.

Junior High School Offense

The plays in *Diagrams 2-7, 2-8, 2-9* and *2-10* make a very fine offense at the Junior High School level. A number of Junior High coaches in the local area have used these plays with the back door movement with great success. It gives the young players a good concept of team offense. The drills in *Diagrams 2-21, 2-22* and others like them help in teaching the offense.

MOTION OR PASSING OFFENSE IN NO-BALL AREA

Everybody is using this offense in one way or another at all levels of basketball today. The main reason for the popularity is that it is a very effective man-to-man offense. With the constant screens and motion within the no-ball area, it is very difficult to keep this offense from getting the 10- to 15-foot uncontested jumper. It is responsible for many teams playing various zone and trap-type defenses today. It is one of the main reasons for the arrival of the multiple defense era. Today there are very few coaches that will play man-to-man against this motion offense for the whole game. This constant movement within such a small area also leads to many illegal screens that the officials hesitate to call. This makes the game rougher and also makes it more difficult for the defense to do a good job.

This offense has most of its screens taking place in the no-ball area. There is constant motion with a combination of down, up and across screens. Some coaches use this offense with a *continuity*. Others use a certain *key* to run a play or series of plays, then when no attempt to score is made, they *reset* to start a new play or series.

Continuity

The continuity type offense is shown in *Diagrams* 2-27 through *2-31*.

Diagram 2-27. Players 3 and 2 screen down, 1 passes to 4, 1 moves to the weak side and screens for 5, 3 moves to the weak side to clear for 5's cut off screen for possible pass from 4.

Diagram 2-28. Player 3, who clears for 5, screens for 2, who moves to the strong side high post on the heels of 5's cut for possible pass from 4.

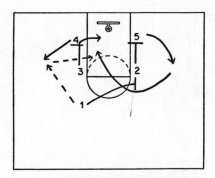

Diagram 2-27

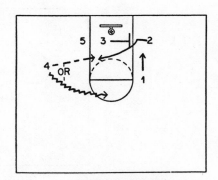

Diagram 2-28

  Diagram 2-29. Player 1 moves down to the low post to help set a double screen for 5 who could receive possible pass from 4.

  Diagram 2-30. Player 2 moves to the point guard position to receive pass from 4, 1 moves across foul lane to low post, 3 moves across the lane to high post, 4 moves to the other high post position.

  Diagram 2-31. Now the offense is ready to start continuity from the other side of the court.

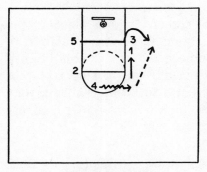

Diagram 2-29

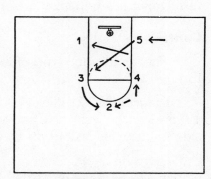

Diagram 2-30

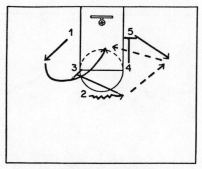

Diagram 2-31

Key Offense

Key—Pass and Go Away
(Same as Diagrams 27 through 31)

This play is determined by what the point guard does after he makes the initial pass. The pattern is determined by 1 *moving away from the ball*. If at the end of this series of plays there has been no attempt to penetrate by a pass or dribble for a shot, 2 starts a new play.

Key—Pass and Follow
(Diagrams 2-32 through 2-36)

Play in *Diagrams* 32 through 36 is keyed by 1 *passing and following*. If there is no break in the pattern, 3 passes back to 1 and the offense resets as shown in *Diagram 36*.

Diagrams 2-32 to 2-33. Players 3 and 2 screen down, 1 passes to 5 and follows, 2 returns to high post, 5 returns ball to 1

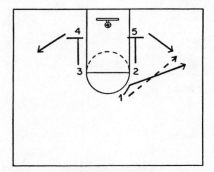

Diagram 2-32

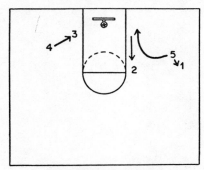

Diagram 2-33

and uses a change up cut to the basket, 1 could pass to 5, 4 starts to move down to set double screen.

Diagram 2-34. Player 2 sets screen for 1, 1 dribbles off 2's screen, 2 rolls toward baseline, 5 moves to weak side using double screen set up by 3 and 4, 1 could pass to 2 or 5.

Diagram 2-35. If 1 cannot pass to 5 or 2, 5 moves out for pass from 1, 3 and 4 move to weak-side low post and set double screen for 2, 5 could pass to 2.

Diagram 2-36. Player 5 returns pass to 1 and team resets for next play.

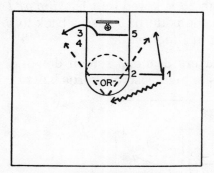

Diagram 2-34

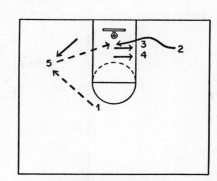

Diagram 2-35

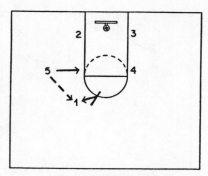

Diagram 2-36

Key—Pass and Stay
(Diagrams 2-37 through 40)

When the defense is very aggressive and pushing the offense out of the desired offensive lanes by their over-play, this *pass and stay* play is a good way to start the offense. It will force the defense to be more careful with their over-play and will help get offense started.

Diagram 2-37. Players 3 and 2 screen down, 1 passes to 4 who has to come all the way back to the guard position to receive pass, because of overaggressive defense player. This keys 1 to *pass and stay.* Player 1 fakes moving away from ball, then flashes back for a return pass from 4.

Diagram 2-38. Player 4 starts moving toward baseline. When 3 and 2 see 1 stay, they immediately flash back to high post; 4 changes direction and moves with them. Player 1 could

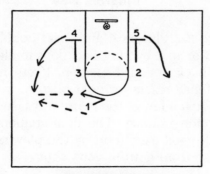

Diagram 2-37

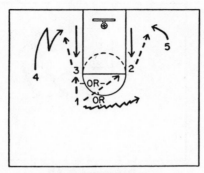

Diagram 2-38

pass to 3 or 2 for back door play to 4 or 5 or he could dribble to his right if he could not pass to 2 or 3.

Diagram 2-39. When 1 dribbles to his right, 3 and 2 screen down for 4 and 5, 1 passes to 5, 4 moves to strong-side low post.

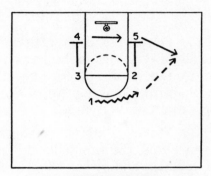

Diagram 2-39

Diagram 2-40. Players 4 and 2 set double screen for 3, 5 could pass to 3 or to 1 cutting backdoor to cleared out area. If not, 5 dribbles back to guard position, 1 returns to backcourt, 5 passes to 1, offense resets for next play.

These are just a few of the many ways the screens are used to run the motion offense. The combinations of screens are many, and with good execution by the players, it is difficult to keep the offense from getting good shots.

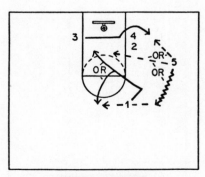

Diagram 2-40

OFFENSE AGAINST MAN-TO-MAN
FULL OR THREE-QUARTER PRESS

One of the best ways to break a full or three-quarter straight man-to-man press is shown in *Diagram 2-41*. Set up any type of screen to get your point guard and best dribbler open for the inbound pass. When the ball is successfully in the point guard's hands, all other players clear out to the front court. Any good dribbler can beat the most accomplished defensive player in getting to the front court. However, this is very tiring for the dribbler and a good aggressive defensive player can work him so hard it may affect the rest of his game. This is the main strategy of most coaches when they use this type of pressing defense. Make the point guard weary and it will upset the whole offense of the opponent. You must have a well-conditioned point guard to handle this type of offense for any length of time. In *Diagram 2-41*, 2 sets screen for 3 then rolls toward ball and receives pass. Everybody clears out and 2 goes one-on-one with his dribble to get to the front court.

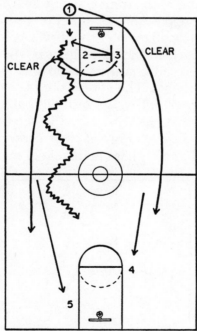

Diagram 2-41

THE FOUR-CORNER OFFENSE

This stall type of offense has been used for years, but only in the 70s did it become known as the *four-corner offense*. Now practically every organized team in basketball uses it as a stall tactic in one way or another. When executed well it can frustrate any defense.

Today's teams may use the four-corner delayed offense at any time during a game. This offense may be used for the whole game, if a team with less talent than their opponent wishes to play a controlled offensive game to keep the score down. Teams have won games using it against highly favored opponents. It is used mostly though for several minutes before the half or near the end of a game to preserve a lead. When the four-corner is used under these circumstances, teams will shoot only the high percentage lay-up shot or short jumper.

The two sets used are shown in *Diagrams* 2-42 and 2-43. Usually in the 3-2 set the guards take turns attempting to penetrate into the center of the front court by beating their men with the dribble. If the opportunity does not present itself for the easy lay-up on the penetration, the guard will hold his dribble and retreat, or pass back to the other guard, who will attempt the same thing. They will continue to do this until they get the close, uncontested shot. The spread out players never stray too far from their corner unless a scoring attempt is being made.

In the 2-1-2 set, 5 is used as the safety valve. The four players, staying in the vicinity of their corner, pass the ball to one another until one of them is unable to make a pass, then 5

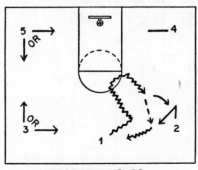

Diagram 2-42

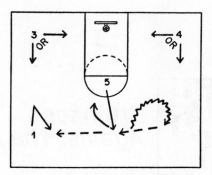

Diagram 2-43

(center) moves out quickly toward the stranded player to receive short pass. This offense is especially successful when the opposing center hesitates to go with him in an attempt to cut off the pass. Most centers will not go out with their man for at least the first two or three times he does this. It is very difficult to force this offense to give the ball up by taking a poor percentage shot or through a turnover. This is especially true if the team has one or two fast, clever dribblers.

SUMMARY

Why are so many teams resorting to the various standard zone defenses or moving one step further and using a multiple defense system? First, they are finding it very difficult to develop a man-to-man defense that is effective against the modern motion and passing offense. The rapidity of the screen, and the constant motion of the offensive players in the no-ball area makes it very difficult to keep the offense from eventually getting the short jumper and other high percentage shots. What makes this offense even more difficult to handle is the inevitable illegal screens that result from the movement in such *close quarters*. The officials seemingly are only able to call the more obvious illegal screens. This has resulted in many coaches resorting to other defenses to stem the tide of this type of offense. The zone defense has become more popular than ever in the high schools and colleges. Many coaches have gone one step further and started using a multiple type defensive system.

3

Offenses Against the Zone

POPULARITY OF ZONES

In the early history of basketball the zone defense became popular when team offense against the man-to-man defenses began to improve. But, that was not the only reason zones were used. Many high schools and colleges played their games on very small basketball courts. The size varied from sixty feet by forty feet to eighty feet by forty feet. Many high schools played on the stage of the school auditorium. Other gyms had balconies that were only ten or fifteen feet high hanging out over the out-of-bounds lines. These balconies would cut off the corner of the courts as much as sixteen feet in some cases. It was impossible to shoot from the corner on this kind of court. A zone defense was very effective on these smaller courts, especially if the offense could not shoot from the corners.

A defense could pack four men in the no-ball area, leaving one man on the ball in the offensive lane. It was a very effective defense in an era when there were few good outside shooters. This defense was especially difficult to penetrate if the defensive players were big.

Dr. John Lawther had this kind of court and players at Westminster College (Pa.) in the late 1920s and early 1930s. His teams became noted for their tough zone defense. When he later moved on to Penn State, where the floor was much bigger and there were no balconies, he was still successful with his zones, but not nearly so much as he had been at Westminster.

Zone defenses are still an important part of basketball in high schools and colleges today. This chapter will show a few of the more productive methods to attack the various zones that are used.

OFFENSES USED AGAINST DIFFERENT ZONES

2-3 Zone

Diagram 3-1 designates the areas of the offensive lane and no-ball area. *Diagram 3-2* shows how the zone sets up when ball is in the *A area*. The *dot* shows the approximate spot where players are located when the ball is in the *B area*. The *point of the arrow* shows their location when the ball is in the *C area*. This defense jams the no-ball area to make penetration difficult. All the slides are generally parallel with the baseline. The back line covers the C and no-ball area and the front line A & B areas.

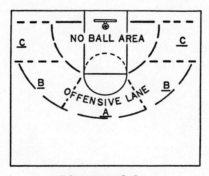

Diagram 3-1

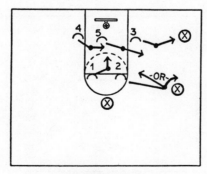

Diagram 3-2

This defense will not attempt to cut off passes in the offensive lane unless it is a careless pass. The player on the ball will stay with the dribbler in the offensive lane until picked up by the player in next area. If the dribbler in *C area* attempts to drive into the no-ball area away from the baseline, 3 will cut off the attempt, which may result in a double team with 3. This same double team (by 2 and 3) may develop if the dribbler tries to penetrate the no-ball area from the *B lane area*. The baseline drive is handled in the same way, with 3 and 5 double-teaming. Player 3 on the ball may double-team, or move on to protect the basket. If there is a pass into the no-ball area from the offensive lane, the attempt for a double team will also occur. The closest defensive man off the ball will double-team. All the good zones will double-team (if they can) once the ball enters the no-ball area, in much the same manner as I have explained to you here.

Aggressive 2-3 Zone

The slides on the aggressive zone are very similar with several exceptions. This zone puts more pressure on the ball in the offensive lane. It has the same basic set, but when the ball is passed from the A to B area, 3 will move out to guard the man with the ball as shown in *Diagram 3-3*. When the ball is passed from B to C area, 2 will drop back to cover the high post, cut off the passing lane to B area, or double-team in the corner. Player 5 covers the ball in C area as 3 moves back to take the medium or low post (*Diagram 3-4*). If 2 cuts off the lane to B area or double-teams, 1 protects the high post. All penetrations toward the

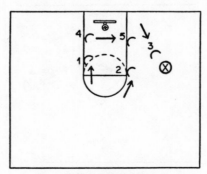

Diagram 3-3

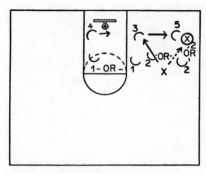

Diagram 3-4

no-ball area are handled in much the same way as in the passive 2-3. However, in the aggressive zone any dribbling in the high C or low B area may be double-teamed.

Proper penetration by good passing and dribbling will get you the necessary good percentage shots to beat this defense. The offense I had the most success with was started from a 1-2-2 set *(Diagram 2-5)*. The outside players pass the ball in the A & B areas as the inside players keep interchanging through the no-ball area keeping the back line defense busy. Many uncontested eighteen to twenty-two foot jumpers can be taken from the *A* and *B* areas. *Deep* penetration by the pass or dribble is difficult. It will create too many turnovers and blocked shots. A pass to the medium post as shown in *Diagram 3-5* is often available; 5 may shoot a jump shot or pass to 4 and 3, depending on how the weakside defense reacts on the pass to 5; 5 may also pass to 2 depending on the strongside defensive reaction. Pene-

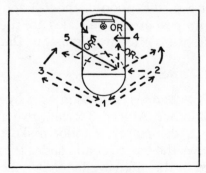

Diagram 3-5

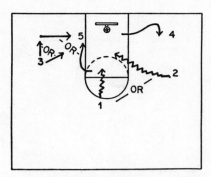

Diagram 3-6

trating the gap with the dribble will also get the good percentage shot, as 1 and 2 do in *Diagram 3-6*. The penetrating guard should stop in the 12- to 15-foot range and go up for the jump shot or the pass off. When the guard begins his penetration, it is the key for the inside men to drop to the low post area or flare out toward the sidelines along the baseline; the outside men to move into any open gap as he penetrates. This offense will get the good 10- to 18-foot "jumper" and will always put at least one player in good position for the rebound. Once the penetration is successful, there is also a good chance to pass off to an inside player for the lay-up as he moves toward the basket along the baseline. Sometimes when the zone over-shifts, a long pass from C or B area (frowned on by many coaches) across court will get you an uncontested 1ɔ- to 18-foot jump shot.

2-1-2 Zone

This is just a modification of the 2-3 zone with 5 moving out to the medium post area. The slides are the same as the 2-3 and the same offense is effective against it *(Diagrams 5 and 6.).*

3-2 and 1-2-2 Zones

The 3-2 or 1-2-2 zones have been used by most every coach at one time or another. A good 3-2 can give any offense problems, especially if the players cannot make the outside shot. *Diagram 3-7* shows the basic set and slides these zones make as the ball is passed in the offensive lane. Dot shows their location when the ball is in the B area. The slides in the 3-2 and 1-2-2 are

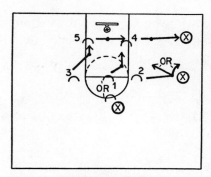

Diagram 3-7

practically the same, only in the 1-2-2, 1 (the point) has a greater area of responsibility. He must be on the ball further out in both the A & B areas in the offensive lane. The 1-2-2 works best when 1 is exceptionally fast with quick hands. The players will stay with the dribble in the offensive lane, until picked up by the player in the next area just like the 2-3 zone. This zone does not double-team often in the offensive lane. They do double-team in the *no-ball area*. The two players on the front line that do not double-team flare out and cut off the passing lanes.

I used a number of offenses against these two zones over the years, but the most successful was a continuity with screens and constant guard movement. We start with a 3-2 set as indicated in *Diagram 3-8*. This continuity was ideal because it kept the two biggest and best inside players in the low and high post area all the time. *Diagrams 8 through 12* show the continuity along with all the planned options within the pattern.

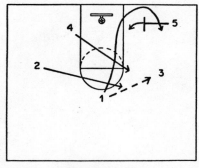

Diagram 3-8

Diagram 3-8. Player 1 passes to 3, then cuts toward the basket; 4 times his move from weak-side low post to strong-side high post on the heels of 1. Player 5 sets a screen for 1. 2 takes 1's place.

Diagram 3-8A. Player 3 could break the pattern here by passing to 1, 5 or 4 as shown. If 3 passes to 4, he could take jumper or pass to 5 or 1.

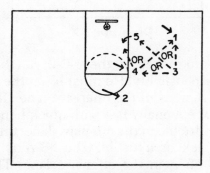

Diagram 3-8A

Diagram 3-9. If 3 does none of the above, he passes back to 2 and cuts immediately across the foul lane to low post area to set a screen for 1. Player 5 moves to high post off 1's heels. Player 1 delays his cut along base-line just long enough for 3 to set the screen. While all this movement is taking place, 2 fakes and dribbles to his left.

Diagram 3-9A. Player 2 could pass to 1, 3 or 5 as shown.

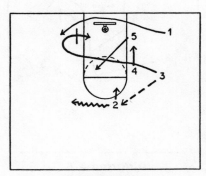

Diagram 3-9

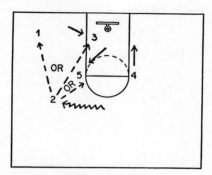

Diagram 3-9A

Diagram 3-10. If 2 does none of the above, 1 moves out to foul line extended to receive the pass from 2. Player 4 drops to the weak-side low post area. Player 3 moves to the weak-side guard position. Player 2 moves toward the weak side.

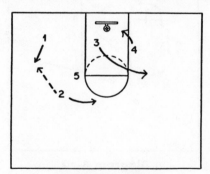

Diagram 3-10

Diagram 3-10A. Player 1 could lob pass to 4, pass to 5, or fake and drive toward the basket for a jump shot or pass off.

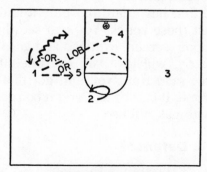

Diagram 3-10A

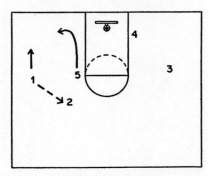

Diagram 3-11

Diagram 3-11. If 1 does none of above, he passes back to 2. They are now ready to start the continuity on the left side of the floor (*Diagram 12*).

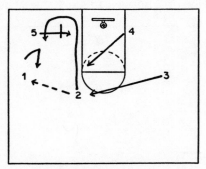

Diagram 3-12

The players knew that when the opportunity was there, they could penetrate the gaps with the dribble for an open shot or pass off to an open player.

Any offense that has guard movement is usually the most successful against these zones. You can see that the above offense has the motion, screen, overload and good balance which, if executed properly, will give you the uncontested shot. Because of the three-man front you can get more close-in shots than on the 2-3 zone. It can be a strong rebounding defense and is suited for a fastbreak offense.

The Modern 3-2 Defense

Diagrams 3-13 through *3-15* show a 3-2 set that coaches have been using off and on for the last decade or so. *This defense*

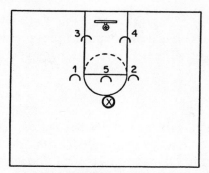

Diagram 3-13

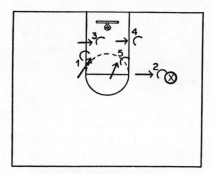

Diagram 3-14

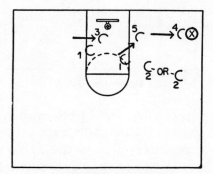

Diagram 3-15

has become more popular in the last few years. The slides are different as you can see. This popularity could be due to the fact that there are more big fast players today. If you have a big, *fast* player it can be an effective defense; 5, the big man, sets up in the center spot on the front line. You can see his slides in the *13 to 15 Diagram series*. You could use both offenses that were illustrated for the 2-3 and the 3-2 zone. Both could be successful against it. Player 5 has a large and important area to cover. With good execution of either of these offenses you could take advantage of this fact.

1-3-1 Zone

This zone has been used with success from the days of Clair Bee, the coach given credit for using it first. The slides used are shown in *Diagram 3-16*. Dot shows where players are located when the ball is in the *B area*. The strength of this zone as you can see is down the center. Player 5 is usually the tallest player on the team and he must cover the same area as 5 did in the 2-1-2 defense: 1 and 4 are kept busy in this zone because they must cover an area of approximately nine feet wide from sideline to sideline. The aggressive 1-3-1 double-teams frequently in the corner.

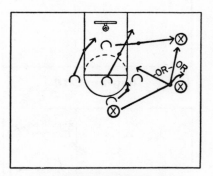

Diagram 3-16

I had a special offense that I used against the 1-3-1. It is a little dangerous because when you have a turnover in this offense you are more susceptible to the fastbreak. I felt it was worth this chance, because we always got good percentage shots when using it. We started out in a 2-3 set with the guards splitting 1, the chaser, and *our forwards and center set low along baseline (Diagram 3-17)*. Our guards would pass back and forth in the offensive lane keeping the 1 chaser busy. If he would stop and split the passing lane, the guard would immediately dribble into the gap between chaser and wing as in *Dia-*

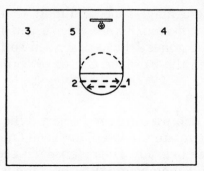

Diagram 3-17

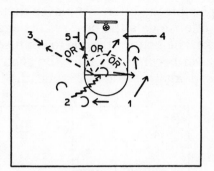

Diagram 3-18

gram 3-18. If 1 didn't split the guards, eventually one of the guards would be able to dribble into the gap. Once penetration was successful, usually one of the three inside men would be open for the high percentage shot. If a pass or shot was not made by the guard penetrating, the other guard would pull back toward the center line to get pass from him. We would then set up again and attempt to do the same thing. Of course, if either guard needed help during any of these maneuvers, 2, 3 and 4 would break up the sidelines and away from baseline to receive the pass. This was all the offense we ever needed against the 1-3-1. Player 5 would always be in the low post area, setting the screens and if open receive a pass for the lay-up. When a shot was taken by teammate, he had good position for the rebound. Players 3 and 4 would be constantly moving back and forth on baseline, coming out toward ball only when help was needed. As I said, a turnover could be trouble, but this offense enabled us to get the good percentage shots and more than made up for the fastbreaks our opponents were able to get. It is interesting to note that all the zones I have described so far have the same alignment when the ball is in C area or corner.

Match-up Zone

A good match-up zone can be very difficult to play against. Fortunately, there are not too many good ones, mainly because it is very difficult to teach. The defense has each player protect a certain area and match up with the various offensive sets as shown in *Diagram 3-19* and *3-20*. Each player will use man-to-man principles on the offensive player that is in his area.

A motion offense gets the best results against a match-up. The more motion the better; it tends to confuse the defense and eventually a player becomes open for the good shot. The motion offense we used against the 3-2 zone did well against the

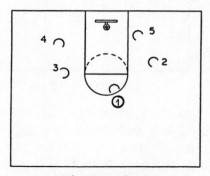

Diagram 3-19

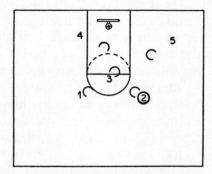

Diagram 3-20

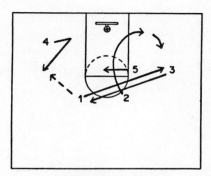

Diagram 3-21

match-up. I also had good success using the man-to-man *shuffle offense* without setting the screens *(Diagram 3-21)*. The constant movement and the players stopping or moving into the unguarded gaps will eventually get the desired shot. Failing to get the desired shot after several rotations within the pattern, a *pass to the player in the high post* keys the offense to break the pattern as shown in *Diagram 3-22*. Player 2 passes to 5, then

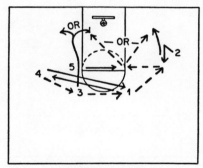

Diagram 3-22

cuts toward the basket. Player 5 could take the jumper or pass to 2 or 3 in the low post on the weak side. *Diagram 3-23* shows 2 continuing the shuffle pattern by passing to 4; 4 passes to 1, 1 breaks the pattern by passing to 5 in the high post. Player 5 could pass to 3, who is moving backdoor toward the basket, or to 2, who stops in the low post area on the weak side. If no shot is taken, set up and start the shuffle again.

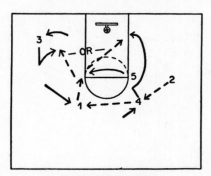

Diagram 3-23

Box & 1, Diamond & 1

These two defenses are designed to put pressure on the super offensive scorer. The best defensive player is assigned to guard the super player and the other four players play zone, either in a 2-2 or 1-2-1 set (*Diagrams 3-24* and *25*). I have seen

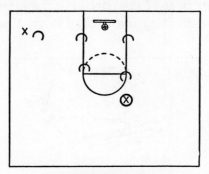

Diagram 3-24

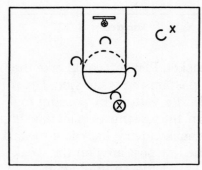

Diagram 3-25

this type of defense upset a top scorer and also do the same thing to the offensive efforts of the rest of the team. When playing against this type of defense, we just used our regular offenses against zones and went to the one that was most successful. I found these defenses, in most cases, to be weak. The strength of these defenses is in the psychological effect they have on the offensive players. By playing our regular offense we found that we could get the good shot. If our top scorer did not maintain his game average, the rest of the players more than made up for it. I believe you get best results against this type of defense by playing an offensive pattern your players are accustomed to.

Triangle & 2

This defense can be difficult especially when your opponent *uses* three big men in the triangle inside the no-ball area. The players in the triangle play zone with the same slides as the 2-3 zone. Just like the 2-3, it is difficult to penetrate for the lay-up. and very strong on the defensive rebounding. The other two players play your guards man-to-man (*Diagram 3-26*). My best offense against this defense was using a three-man interchange in the offensive lane. We would have our best outside shooting forward play the third guard position. If you don't pull the zone out by bringing this third man out to guard, you must hit the 15- to 20-foot jumper to be successful against this defense. With the three man zone positioned in the no-ball area, it is not difficult to get this shot. Players 4 and 5 keep the triangle busy by interchanging along the baseline and medium post area. Rather than the guards passing back and forth in the offensive lane until they have an opportunity to penetrate with the dribble as in the 2-3 zone offense, the three guards will interchange (*Diagram 3-26*). If this doesn't pull one of the players in the triangle out, the guards will easily get the 15- to 18-foot jumper. Two men cannot guard three. This interchange eventually gets 1, 2 or 3 open in the lower half of the offensive lane for the uncontested jumper. If these three hit this jump shot, one of the defensive men in the triangle must come out. Once you force one of the players in the triangle to come out to help, this defense begins to lose its effectiveness.

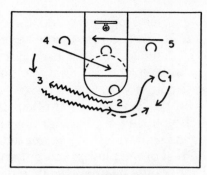

Diagram 3-26

1-2-1-1 Full Court Zone Press

The 1-2-1-1 is a press that features the double team. When the ball is pushed down the side lines, it can be a series of double teams from baseline to baseline. In recent years the double team has become a very popular defensive manuever. When executed properly it will slow up the good passer and dribbler and play havoc with a planned offense.

You must have a well-planned offense against this defense or it will create many costly turnovers. The best offenses will attempt to get the inbound pass into the center of the court or over the top of the first line of defense. The basic set of the defense is shown in *Diagram 3-27. Diagrams 3-27* through *3-31* will illustrate a few of the better ways to attack this defense.

Since there are various ways in which a 1-2-1-1 defense applies pressure in the backcourt, the offense used must be flexible. A 4-1 offense (four in the backcourt and one in the frontcourt) is one of the better offenses to use against this defense because of its adjustability. *Diagram 3-27* shows X^4 being able to receive a pass in the foul line area because defensive players 2 and 3 moved with X^2 and X^3 and defensive player 4 did not attempt to follow him. If X^4 can pass over the front line defense the press is broken.

Diagram 3-27A shows X^4 was unable to pass to either X^2 or X^3. If X^4 also is unable to dribble down the center, he passes back to X^1. X^1 then attempts to dribble into the center or pass to X^4. If either X^1 or X^4 runs into trouble X^3 comes back to help. If you are able to keep the ball away from the sidelines, the chance of having a turnover is minimized.

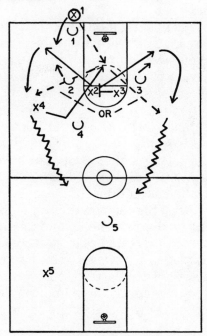

Diagram 3-27

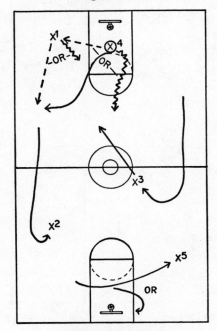

Diagram 3-27A

If the defense is making it difficult for X⁴ to receive the ball
in the foul lane area, an adjustment in the offense is necessary.
Diagram 3-28 shows X³ from the same basic set step out-of-
bounds and receive a pass from X¹. X³passes inbound to X¹ or
X⁴. The one who receives the pass will attempt to dribble down
the center. If either has trouble they may pass to X² in the
frontcourt or pass back to X³ who is the safety valve. *This pass
out-of-bounds to X³ is only legal after a field goal or foul.*

If you're still having trouble, you can always get the pass
inbounds by passing into the corner, because that's where the
defense wants you to pass it. Most of these 1-2-1-1 defenses will
play one of their fastest big men on the ball to make the inbound
pass more difficult and also to be able to use his height on the
double team when the inbound pass goes to the corner. However, if it does happen, a turnover may be avoided by proper
positioning of the offensive players. In *Diagram 3-29* defensive
players 3 and 4 must cover three men. With the offensive
players positioned as shown, one of the three offensive players

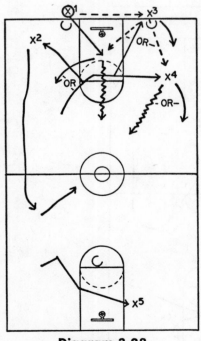

Diagram 3-28

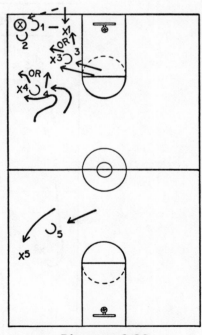

Diagram 3-29

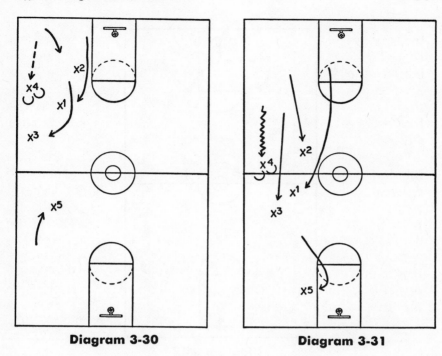

Diagram 3-30 **Diagram 3-31**

X^1, X^3, or X^4 will be open for the pass, depending on who 3 and 4 decide to guard.

Once the offense is past the front line defense, it must move quickly into the front court and when possible stay away from the sidelines. If the offense moves too slow and has the ball near the sideline, the defense will set up another double team as shown in *Diagrams 3-30* and *3-31*. Any pass out of a double team to the weak side is too long and dangerous and should not be thrown. It is recommended that the offensive players off the ball remain in the general positions shown. X^4 must be sure he doesn't cross the centerline (*Diagram 3-31*) when he sees the double team forming. If he does cross it, he is now unable to pass back to X^2. He has lost one avenue of breaking the trap.

2-2-1 Three-Quarter Zone Press

The basic set of this defense is shown in *Diagram 3-32*. The big play in all pressing defenses is forcing the offense into a turnover. This is also true with the 2-2-1, but most coaches'

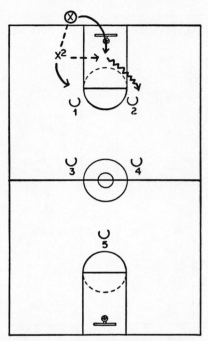

Diagram 3-32

main desire in this defense is to slow the quick transition of the opponent in moving the ball to the front court. The 1 and 2 defensive players fake at guard with the ball and then drop back and at the same time try to force the dribble or pass down the sideline. This whole defense just keeps sliding back, staying with the basic set you see in *Diagram 3-32*. If they are successful in pushing the ball to the sideline, they will attempt to double-team as shown in *Diagram 3-33*. They will try to execute the double team, when the opportunity presents itself, from the spot illustrated in *Diagram 3-33* all the way along the sidelines to the deep corner.

One of the better offenses against this defense is shown in *Diagram 3-34*. The guard with the ball should dribble right at the front line of the defense, then with short passes move the ball back and forth with other guard until X^3 breaks into heart of the defense. If X^1 passes to X^3 as the zone collapses on him, X^3 can now pass to X^1 who is moving quickly down the side ahead of the defense. If the 3 defensive man plays X^3 tight, 1 may pass over the defense to X^4, who has moved into backcourt to the area

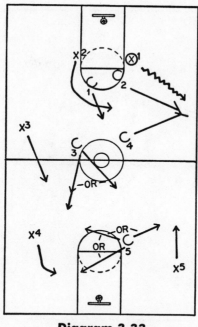

Diagram 3-33

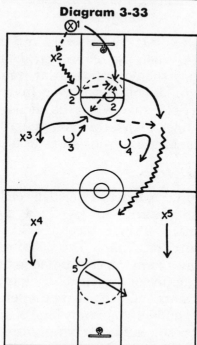

Diagram 3-34

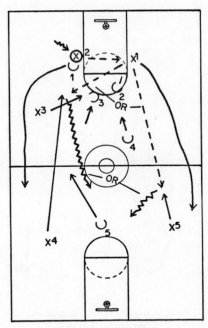

Diagram 3-35

X³ left (*Diagram 3-35*). If defensive player 5 moves up with X⁴, X¹ can pass to X⁵. When the offense breaks through the front defensive line, they should dribble away from the sidelines as shown. If the offense is able to stay away from the sidelines, this defense is not very effective. When the offense gets ahead of the defensive front line, many three-on-one situations develop. These fast breaks lead to uncontested, good percentage shots.

1-3-1 Half Court Trap

This half court trap defense is usually called the 1-3-1 trap, but its set is as shown in *Diagram 3-36*. It attempts to accomplish the same thing as the full court 1-2-1-1 press does, but from the half court positioning. The defense will double-team down both side lines from the center line to the baseline and at the same time attempt to cut off all the passing lanes. If the double team forces the offense to pass the soft lob passes of any distance, it is very difficult to get any kind of an effective offense started. This will result in too many turnovers, which is exactly what the defense is trying to produce.

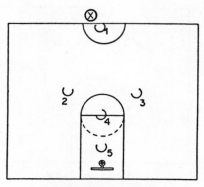

Diagram 3-36

The best offense is to use as few perimeter passes as possible and penetrate to the heart of the defense with the dribble or pass as soon as the opportunity presents itself. *Diagram 3-37* shows one of the ways to do this. As soon as X^1 sees 2 defensive man move up to double-team, he makes a *short* pass to X^3. When X^3 receives pass, he immediately dribbles toward the no-ball area. After penetration, X^3 may pass to X^1, X^5, or X^4, or he may take a jump shot (*Diagram 3-38*). If a shot does not result from this penetration, the ball is passed back to open guard and the offense sets up again to get same type of penetration.

If 1 defensive player decides to split the passing lanes between X^1 and X^2 rather than double team as shown in *Diagram 3-39*, the gap is now open for a pass to X^4 if he is open; if not, X^2 moves out, X^1 passes to X^2, X^2 passes back to X^1. Now the gap is

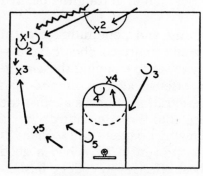

Diagram 3-37

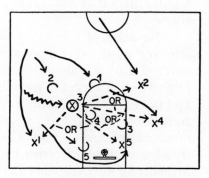

Diagram 3-38

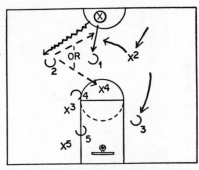

Diagram 3-39

open for X^1 to dribble into the center as X^4 and X^3 clear out toward respective sidelines. 1 can now pass to X^3, X^5, or X^4. This penetrating offense avoids excessive passing on the perimeter and does not use the long cross court pass. Proper execution in this type of offense will get the good percentage shot and cut down the turnovers. It will also prevent the defense from using the double team trap as often as they would like. This penetrating offense keeps the man with the ball from getting too close to the sidelines and away from the corners where the double team is most dangerous.

SUMMARY

This chapter has given a brief explanation of most of the zone defenses that have been used in basketball up to the present. There are a number of different offenses that are successful against each of these defenses. The offenses explained here are the ones that I found did the best job in getting the desired shots.

Because of the many screening and penetrating type of offenses used today against the zone, many coaches have discovered the zone alone is not the answer to stopping these ever-improving offenses. The motion offense against man-to-man and the effective screening and penetrating offenses against the zone have brought more coaches into experimenting with a multiple defense system. The following chapters will explain in detail a multiple defense that has proven to have had a good measure of success against the best offenses in college basketball.

PART II
THE AMOEBA DEFENSE

4

Man-to-Man Defense in the Offensive Lane

TEACHING METHOD

I found that the best way to teach the front court man-to-man defense was by the use of a floor chart (*Diagrams 4-1* and *4-1A*). The floor is divided within this radius into the following areas. The *no-ball* area is a 15-foot radius around the basket. The 10 feet between the No-Ball area and the 25 foot perimeter is called the *offensive lane*. This lane is the area in which the offense sets up patterns or moves in order to penetrate the no-ball area or get the good shot in the lane. The lane is divided into five areas. *A* is in the center from the foul line to four feet above the foul circle; *B* is on each side of *A*; *C* is in each corner. How the defensive player plays his man is determined by the *number of passes* his man is away from the ball by using the

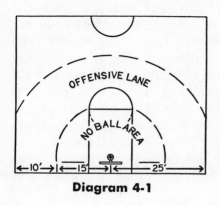

Diagram 4-1

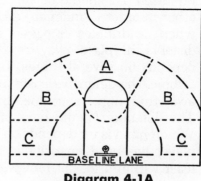

Diagram 4-1A

lane route or *path*. For example, if the ball is located in one of the C areas; strong side B is *one* pass away; A is *two* passes away; weak side B is *three* passes away; and weak side C is *four* passes away. Another example—if the ball is in one of the B areas; strong side C is *one* pass away; A is *one* pass away; weak side B is *two* passes away; weak side C is *three* passes away. The no-ball area is only *one* pass from the ball in any of the five lane areas. Each area in the lane represents one pass.

This area system in teaching the front court man-to-man defense gives the player a better understanding of how he should guard his man in each of the five following situations in the offensive lane area:

1. Defensing the man with the ball.
2. Defensing the man one pass away.
3. Defensing the man two passes away.
4. Defensing the man three passes away.
5. Defensing the man four passes away.

DEFENSING THE MAN WITH THE BALL

When guarding the man with the ball no certain stance is required as long as the player maintains good balance with his knees bent, head up, tail down, and as long as he is ready to move in any direction. Both the "boxer" and "parallel" stances are accepted, so the player should use whichever one is more comfortable for him. As a player, I always felt most comfortable with my right foot forward in a boxer stance. As a coach, I decided that it was best to let the player decide which method he preferred. He should be shifting his weight from one foot to the other in order to maintain good position on the offensive player when he dribbles or passes and cuts toward the basket. The distance he plays away from his man when he is not moving depends on several things. If the offensive player still has his dribble, the defensive position should be from *two* to *three* feet away from him, determined by the *speed* of the offensive player. The defender should have one hand up and one hand down. Which hand is up depends on the player himself. If the offensive player has used his dribble, the defensive player should be at least within a foot of him with both arms flaring making it as difficult as possible to shoot or pass. He should not slap or reach for the ball at the expense of losing good defensive position. He should not reach across in front or back of the offensive player in an attempt to steal the ball. If the offensive player places the ball in a position where trying to steal the ball will not likely create a foul, the player may take a chance. When he does attempt to dislodge the ball from an opponent, he should reach for the ball with both hands or slap at it with an *upward motion*. The chances of fouling are too great when slapping down at the ball. Only a player with exceptionally quick hands can get away with slapping down on the ball. When you do have a player like that, he can be successful with the downward motion when the ball is in position for an easy steal. Whether the initial stance in guarding the man with the ball is head-on or a little to his left or right depends on—(1) The scouting report; and (2) the defensive strategy for that particular game. This will be explained later.

How to defense the man immediately after he passes or shoots while in the lane area is a very important part of the total front court man-to-man defense. A good offensive player does one of two things after he shoots the ball from the *lane area*. He may retreat a few steps preparing to go on defense or he may follow his shot in an attempt to get the rebound. After the shot has been released, the defensive player should wait to see what the shooter plans to do. If he attempts to follow his shot, the defensive player's job is to block him out before attempting to help on the rebound. This can best be done by a reverse pivot, holding the opponent off for a split second, then releasing. If he does not follow his shot, the defensive man should still move toward the area he is responsible for on the rebound.

REBOUND DRILL FOR BLOCKING-OUT SHOOTER

One ball is used in this drill. All the other "shooters" go through the motion of shooting without the ball. The defensive player should get the ball if it rebounds into his area of responsibility. Each player plays the ball as though his man shot it. The shooters, *without faking*, try to follow their shot for the rebound. The defensive players block-out their men with a reverse pivot, then move to their assigned area for rebound (*Diagram 4-2*). In

Diagram 4-2

explaining how to make a reverse pivot, it is less confusing to your players if you tell them *to pivot so their body is moving toward the opponent's basket.* If the ball rebounds into their area they should get it. After all players have been on defense in each group, they rotate in a clockwise manner. The same group always shoots the ball. This gives them practice on shots taken from different locations in the lane area.

This block-out fundamental *is neglected by most players in the lane area unless you insist on it.* This drill helps them to remember to do it in a game situation. It is important that the offensive player *does not fake* one way and go the other. The main idea in this drill is to teach the defensive player the fundamentals of blocking-out and then covering the proper area for a long rebound.

REBOUND DRILL FOR BLOCKING-OUT AWAY FROM THE BALL

In *Diagram 4-3* the players get practice on blocking-out in the lane area when their man is one to four passes away from the ball. The coach shoots the ball from *A, B* or *C* lane areas. They should open up toward the ball when guarding a man away from the ball. Sometimes this requires a reverse pivot, other times a forward pivot. Players should try never to turn their back on the flight of the ball when preparing to block-out a man away from the ball.

The same drill is used for the inside men guarding the

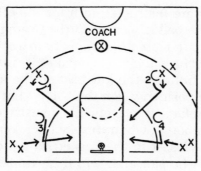

Diagram 4-3

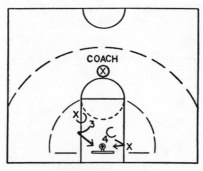

Diagram 4-4

offensive player in the high or low post (*Diagram 4-4*). The coach shoots from the lane areas. If the shot is from the *A* and *B* areas, the defensive players are to use a closed stance from the inside or outside depending on the location of the shot. To block-out properly, they must move the foot closest to the baseline about six inches to a foot toward the baseline and then use a reverse pivot. From a closed stance, this is the best method to get between the basket and the offensive man. *In a closed stance, the defensive player has one foot and an extended arm between the ball and his man*; 3 would have his right foot and right arm in this position, 4 would have his left foot and left arm in this position. Since 4 is guarding the man in the low post and the ball is in the *A* area, he is splitting his man, although using a closed stance. When the shot is taken he must slide back quickly and then use a reverse pivot to block him out.

The players are instructed to front the offensive player in the low post if the ball is located in the C area. *In fronting the man, the whole body facing the ball is in direct line between the ball and the offensive player.* This makes it very difficult for the defensive player fronting the low post on the strong side to get good rebounding position when the ball is shot from the C area. The weak-side defensive players are instructed to help out on the strong-side rebound when this shot is taken. The weak-side defensive player closest to the basket should cross over to the strong side when he can and help if he thinks the rebound is coming down on that side. *Diagram 4-5* illustrates the movement of the defensive players from the weak side when the shot is taken from the corner. Any player in the foul lane or weak side area should help on short rebounds when able to do so.

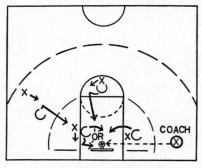

Diagram 4-5

DEFENSING PLAYER AFTER HE PASSES

After the player passes, he may do one of the following: (1) stand still; (2) move toward the ball; (3) move away from the ball; (4) cut toward the basket.

No matter what the offensive player does, the immediate reaction of the defensive player is to move *one to two steps back and toward the direction of the pass.* He is now ready to defend any move his opponent makes. *This is one of the most important fundamentals in man-to-man defense.* Many players will not do this unless you drill them often enough on the move so that it becomes a reflex action. The failure of the defensive players to take those two steps has made the give and go play one of the most successful against the man-to-man defense. *Incidentally, the pros are surprisingly weak on this fundamental.*

Drills

If the passer moves toward the ball, the defensive player uses a closed stance moving in front of his intended path forcing him to go *back door (Diagram 4-6).* When a defensive player forces his man to go backdoor, *he is keeping his body between the ball and his man.* If he is successful, he remains in this closed position concentrating completely on his man until the offensive player in his move toward the basket is about to enter the foul lane area. At this time, the defensive player opens up to the ball, using a *reverse pivot.* He now concentrates on the ball, stays in the lane area and waits until his man changes direction to move either to the weak side or to the strong side. If his man moves to the strong side, the defensive man returns to the closed stance position. If he moves to the weak side, the defensive player uses an *open stance* and *splits* the passing lane between the ball and his man. He places himself in such a position that he may see both the ball and his man. He remains near enough to his man so that if a crosscourt pass is made to him he will be able to intercept, or at least be within three or four feet of his man by the time the pass reaches him. *An open stance is the position where the defensive player can see both his man and the ball location without turning his head.* He must use his peripheral vision. *Splitting the passing lane means the defensive*

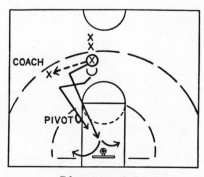

Diagram 4-6

player off the ball moves away from the player he is guarding to a position between the ball and his man. How far away from his man is determined by his speed and the distance his man is from the ball.

When a passer fakes moving toward the ball and cuts *directly toward the basket,* the defensive man must stay between the ball and his man using a closed position and concentrating all his efforts on his man until he enters the foul lane area, and then the defensive man opens up toward the ball using a *reverse pivot (Diagram 4-7).* I believe that any time one of the defensive players is forced to *run* after his man in the offensive lane defense, he has been beaten by him. If the player uses the reverse pivot, he should never have to run after his man. By using this pivot he can always use the proper slide and glide fundamentals to stay with his man. Another reason for the reverse pivot is that the defender will never turn his back on the ball when pivoting to open up to the ball.

In this defense, the only time the defensive player loses complete sight of the ball is when the offensive player is taking his first three or four steps toward the foul lane. The only time the defensive player loses complete sight of his man is the first three or four steps after the man is in the foul lane. Keeping complete concentration on the player for these first few steps will stop the defensive player from opening up to the ball too soon. *This opening up too soon is a common error in guarding the man without the ball.* As soon as the offensive player moves toward the weak side or strong side from the foul lane, the

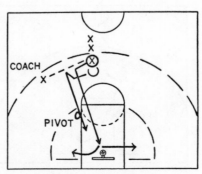

Diagram 4-7

defensive player should be in a position where he can see both his man and the ball.

When the passer moves away from the ball, the defensive player does not go with his man, but slides back into the foul lane area opening his stance until by using his peripheral vision, he can see both his man and the ball *(Diagram 4-8)*. He splits the passing lane between the ball and his man in a way that allows him to get to his man if the ball is passed to him. If the passer sets up a screen for a teammate on the weak side and the teammate cuts off the screen moving toward the lane area or strong side, the defender calls out "switch" and takes the new man, attempting to force him away from the no-ball area or to take the backdoor route. By sagging back, he also helps to make it difficult for a pass to any other offensive player who may be stationed or moving through the no-ball area.

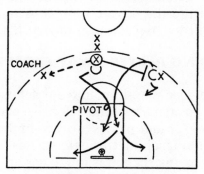

Diagram 4-8

Drills can help players learn the foot-work necessary to defense these moves successfully. These drills make the players realize the importance of moving a step or two back and in the direction of the pass as soon as the pass leaves the player's hands. He finds out he can handle the passer's cut toward the basket or his move toward the ball much easier when he follows this simple rule. When the passer makes his backdoor move, the defensive player must prevent the coach from passing the ball to him as he moves toward the basket. The coach will only pass the ball when the player is doing a poor job in defensing his man. *When the passer goes away from the ball,* this drill helps the player realize the logic in moving to the position requested.

Splitting the ball and the man with an open stance, he can handle the job of guarding his man and still protect the vulnerable foul lane area. Since, in most man-to-man offenses, when the passer moves away from the ball he usually sets a screen for a teammate, the defensive player also gets good practice making this important switch. Good defensive players learn to *talk* and the drill gives them practice doing it. When the coach does not pass the ball, the offensive player moves out of the foul lane to the weak side or strong side. If he moves to the strong side, the defensive player picks him up using a closed stance. If he moves to the weak side, he uses an open stance and splits the ball and his man.

The coach will move to all five offensive lane areas during this drill. *The main purpose of this drill is to teach the proper foot work and positioning for when the passer makes his move from the lane area.* Therefore, we instruct the offensive player to go backdoor toward the basket as soon as the defensive player makes it difficult for him to move toward the ball.

GUARDING PLAYER AWAY FROM THE BALL

The key to good man-to-man team defense in the offensive lane area is the positioning of the defensive player when his man is one, two, three, or four passes away from the ball. This is why the area system in teaching this defense has been so helpful. In using this system, instruction is much easier. The players seem to get a better understanding of their responsibilities. This is especially true of the young, inexperienced player. Even the *9- to 12-year-old players* are able to learn positioning from this teaching system.

Ball in A Area

Diagram 4-9 shows the ball in the A area. It is one pass away from the B and the no-ball area. It is two passes away from the C area. *Diagram 4-9* illustrates how to guard the man in each area. Players 2 and 3 (one pass away) use a closed stance and overplay their men, trying to make it difficult for them to receive a pass. A *closed stance is the position where the defensive player has turned his back on the ball, but turns his head to*

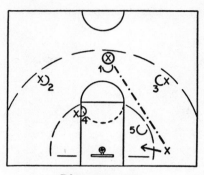

Diagram 4-9

employ his peripheral vision. He can then see his man *and* the offensive player with the ball. Player 2 has his right foot forward and his right hand, with the *thumb down,* extending so that it is between his man and the ball. If he rests his chin against the shoulder of the arm that is extended, he will be able to keep his sight on both his man and the ball. Player 3 is guarding his man in the same way, only his left foot is up and his left hand is extended. Both try to keep their men from moving toward the ball in the lane area. They are always alert and ready for the backdoor move. Player 4 is in the *no-ball area* also only one pass away. Player 4 uses the same closed stance, and since the ball is in the *A* area, he overplays his man from the inside position. Player 5's man is two passes away in the *C* area; therefore, he splits his man using an open stance. In order that 5 can easily see both his man and the ball using his peripheral vision, he must be from two to four feet behind an imaginary straight line between his man and the ball. This is the *ball-you-man* position in man-to-man defense. The imaginary line is shown on *Diagram 4-9.* If 5's man moved into the no-ball area as the arrow indicates on the diagram, 5 would change to a closed stance as his man now would be only one pass away.

Ball in B Area

In *Diagram 4-10,* the ball is located in the *B* area. Player 2's man is only one pass away in the *A* area, but in the *A* and *B* areas, if the offensive player is further away from the baseline than the player with the ball, the defensive player *does not* use a

Diagram 4-10

closed stance. He drops away from his man toward the ball in an open stance. This is to help 1 if 1's man tries to drive toward the no-ball area. *This is the only time in the man-to-man lane defense when the ball is "one pass away" that the players do not use a closed stance.* However, if 1's man passes the ball back to 2's man, he must move out quickly and play him tight and attempt to push him out of the offensive lane. Defensive player 3's man is in the weak side B area, two passes away. Player 3 splits the ball and his man slides toward the foul lane area. The more speed a defensive player has, the more he can "cheat" (move further away from his man) when his man is two, three, or four passes away. Player 4's man is at the high post in the no-ball area, so he uses a closed stance on the left side (outside position). This is the most difficult defensive position to handle in a man-to-man defense. Unless the defensive player is constantly alert and quick to react, he will get caught out of position when the ball is passed from the A to B area and then into the high post. When the ball is passed from A to B area, *he has to move from the inside to the outside position.* If his back foot is closer to the baseline than the offensive player, a reverse pivot and roll to the baseline side is the best method. But if he is too far in front of his man, the best method is to go over the top away from the baseline. Player 5's man is three passes away in weak side C and he should slide into the foul lane area with an open stance. Player 5 is always ready to help if they try to lob the ball to 4's man. He has the dual responsibility when in this position of (1) guarding his man, and (2) protecting the basket area. If

5's man moves into the *no-ball area* to receive a pass, he is now only *one pass* away and 5 must guard him with a *closed stance.*

Ball in C Area

The ball is located in the *C* area *(Diagram 4-11)*. Player 2's man is only one pass away in the *B* area. Player 2 will use a closed stance with the left foot forward and his left hand extended, but he will drop off his man six to nine feet, splitting his man and the ball. He makes it difficult for his man to go toward the ball and for the player with the ball to pass it back to his man. He is always ready for the back door move toward the basket. The *arrow* shows the back door move in this situation. Player 4 splits his man as shown in the diagram. Player 3 uses a closed stance in the post area, with the left hand extended and left foot forward, forcing his man to go backdoor if he moves toward the basket. The arrow in the diagram shows the move. Player 5's man is four passes away, so he splits his man and protects the basket area using an open stance. He moves as close to the strong side as his quickness will let him. If a long pass is made across the court to his man, he must be able to cover him.

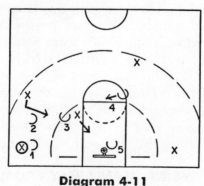

Diagram 4-11

Ball in No-Ball Area

Although we call the 15-foot radius around the basket the no-ball area, we know that our opponents are going to penetrate it. When the ball is in this area, we must do our best to keep the offense from having easy and uncontested shots.

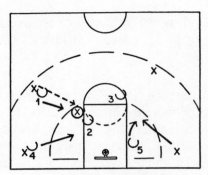

Diagram 4-12

Diagram 4-12 illustrates our defense alignment when the offensive player has the ball in this area. When a pass is made from the B area to the man in the post area (2's man), numbers 3, 5, and 4 split their men and attempt to cut off the passing lanes to their offensive player and at the same time must be ready to help 2 if his man makes a move toward them with a dribble. *This is the "help and recovery" move.* The defensive man off the ball moves in such a way to help a teammate when his man is trying to penetrate defense by use of the dribble. He slows or stops the dribbler, then immediately returns to his own man. Player 1 will double-team with 2 whenever possible. If 2's man had received the ball in the low post on the strongside, 4 would have helped with the double team because he would have been closer to the ball than 1. Once the ball is in this area, the defense must confine the movement of the man with the ball as much as possible. It is *imperative* that the man with the ball in this area is *double-teamed*. If not, even the average offensive ball player will get a good shot or pass off to a teammate who has a better one. Defending the shot will be explained later.

DRILL DEFENSING MAN AWAY FROM THE BALL

The coach has the ball in this drill. He begins in the *A* area as shown in *Diagram 4-13*. The offensive player is in the *B* area. Since he is only one pass away, the defensive player is guarding him with a closed stance. The offensive player, running at *half speed*, moves to all the other areas. He will first try to go toward the ball and the defensive player will move in front of him forc-

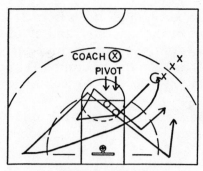

Diagram 4-13

ing him backdoor. The offensive player now moves through the no-ball area to the *C* area, *stops for a second,* then moves from the *C* area into the high post, *stops for a second,* then moves to the strong side *C, stops for a second,* then moves back to the *B* area. The coach mostly just fakes the pass. He is primarily concerned with teaching the defensive player the proper defensive position he should be in as the offensive player moves from one pass away, through the no-ball area to two passes away, and then back to the high post, and then to two passes away again, and finally back to one pass away.

The coach will move to all five areas in the lane before the drill is over. Each defensive player will have practice with the proper position he should assume when the pass is one, two, three, or four passes away.

When the defensive player is not moving the way he should, the coach will pass the ball to the offensive player to keep him alert. When the defensive player knows that the coach may pass the ball at any time, he tends to run this drill in the manner expected in a game.

CHECK POINTS ON DEFENSE WITH DRILLS

At the college level to drill just for drill's sake could be wasted time. Therefore, most of these drills are developed from game situations. The drills used to teach the players the proper skills in the front court man-to-man defense are determined by the answer to the following question. How many ways may an opponent get the ball into the good shooting percentage area?

The good shooting percentage area is from 21 feet to the lay-up. This includes part of the lane area and all of the no-ball area. There are seven ways the opponent may get the ball into this area; (1) pass; (2) dribble; (3) rebound; (4) jump ball; (5) loose ball; (6) foul; and (7) recovery. We call these the *seven check points on defense.*

Drills on the pass and defensive rebound have been shown. Following are the drills on the other five check points.

The Dribbler

In this drill the defensive player guards the dribbler from one end of the court to the other *(Diagram 4-14)*. The defensive player must keep his hands behind his back. He must not let the dribbler get ahead of him. This will help the player on his foot work in guarding the dribbler. The dribbler should attempt to beat the defensive player, but when he does, slow up and let the defensive player get good position again and so on down the floor. If the dribbler does not try to beat him, the drill could be a waste of time.

Diagram 4-14

Dribbler Entering the No-Ball Area

In this drill the defensive player tries to keep the dribbler from entering the no-ball area. The dribbler must try to move into the no-ball area without turning and backing into the defensive player. Also he must accomplish this drive in *five dribbles* or less (*Diagram 4-15*).

Diagram 4-16 shows a drill on how the defensive players get practice guarding the player when he stops his dribble in the front court. They also get practice guarding the man away from the ball. As soon as the dribbler stops in the *A* area, the defensive man moves in close to him with *arms* flaring. There may be three, four, or five offensive men and defensive men in this drill. The dribbler *must stop* in one of the lane areas; *A, B* or *C*. All the defensive players away from the ball must use a preventive (closed) stance on their men to make the pass difficult. This drill makes the players very conscious of the overplay on their men when the offensive player stops the dribble in or near the lane

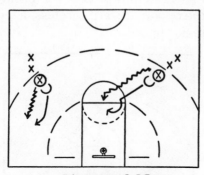

Diagram 4-15

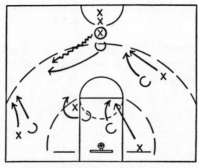

Diagram 4-16

area. The defensive player will overplay his man even when he moves out beyond the 25-foot perimeter in an attempt to get open for the pass from his teammate. This overplay, when the player stops his dribble, is a must. This is one of the best times to force a poor pass. If you do not have a drill on overplay when the dribbler stops, many players will fail to be alert for it in a game situation.

The Jump Ball

When there is a jump ball in the defensive foul lane area, consider the three possibilities that any jump ball presents: (1) should get the tip; (2) tip could go either way; (3) should not get the tip. *Diagram 4-17* shows the formation and movement if we "should get the tip." This is the general position of the players on the jump ball; 1 may tip the ball to 2, 4, or 3, depending on the positions of the opponent's players. The players must be defensive minded on a jump ball here. Player 3's move toward the opponent's basket will help 5 protect the basket if they happen to get the tip. If the opponents are careless, a long tip to 4 makes for a good fastbreak opportunity.

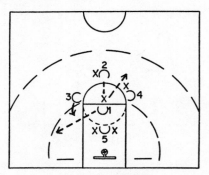

Diagram 4-17

When we "should not get the tip" or it "could go either way," we think mainly of the defensive aspect of the jump ball (*Diagram 4-18*). Players 4 and 5 will try to discourage the tip by the opponent to X2 by moving in tight on both sides. Our 3 man will move to the defense as the ball is tipped to help the 5 and 4 men defense the no-ball area. Our 2 man plays in a way that can help 4 defense X3 if the ball is tipped to him. Player 2 may even

Diagram 4-18

steal the tip if the jumper is not accurate with the tip or X3 is not aggressive in receiving it. The jumper will try to make the long tip to the 3 man as he goes back on defense or to 2 if he feels he can get it to him. Many coaches do not spend enough time on the jump ball. This is one of the little things that can make the difference in a close game. Regardless of the jump ball situation, at least *one player is always reacting defensively.* An opponent should *never* score off a jump ball. We also tried to have one player free in an attempt to steal the tip controlled by the opponents.

Loose Ball

The recovery of a loose ball in this area is very important. Players are encouraged to leave their feet if it is necessary in getting a loose ball. An important aspect of recovering a loose ball in this area is that it may give you an easy field goal. A loose ball recovery is one of the best chances for a successful fast break and score. The opponents are often caught with no one back and the fast break leads to an easy field goal. We used a drill to teach our players to look immediately for the fastbreak possibility when they gain possession of a loose ball.

The coach rolls the ball on the floor somewhere in the no-ball area, a player moves in and picks up the ball and another player breaks down the floor for a long pass *(Diagram 4-19)*. The pass is thrown ahead of the player so that he runs into it on the way for a lay-up. The long lob pass should come down to the floor near *the top of the key area*. On recovering a loose ball, the player must always look toward his own basket for a possible

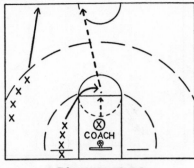

Diagram 4-19

fastbreak situation. This type of pass has to be practiced if you expect your players to do it in the regular games.

Foul Prevention

When you foul an opponent, you are letting him get the highest percentage shot in the game with the exception of the uncontested lay-up. Fouls must be kept to a minimum. This is one of the biggest problems a coach has in teaching a good, *aggressive* defense. How can you be aggressive and still keep fouling to a minimum? More fouls are called on the defensive man when he is guarding the man with the ball than in any other situation. Most fouls are created by the hands. The drills on guarding the man with the ball emphasize that if the player uses his feet, hands, and body properly he need not foul unnecessarily.

When the defensive man is guarding the man with the ball *outside the 25-foot* perimeter in the back court or the front court, the defensive player should keep his hands low, palms up. He must only slap at the ball with an upward motion or reach for it with both hands in an attempt to make a steal. He must do this only when the ball is between him and an offensive player; in other words, only when the offensive player gets careless in his ball handling or dribbling. His feet must move in such a way as to keep his body between the offensive player and the area the defensive player wishes to penetrate. This can only be done by keeping the knees bent, body low and ready to move into the slide and glide method used by all good defensive players. He must *never* try to reach across or around the back of the body to slap the ball away from the dribbler. This maneuver should only be used in a desperate situation, when you are behind near the end of a game. These fundamentals can be practiced when using the drill shown in *Diagram 4-14*.

When the defensive man is guarding the man with the ball in the lane area, the same stance is used but with one hand extended upward within one to two feet of his face to help harass the pass or shot. The other hand is kept low to keep good balance and a better position if he tries to dribble into the no-ball area. The defensive player should not jump to block the shot, if the player still has his dribble. When guarding a player who attempts to shoot off his dribble in the lane area, the player should jump in an attempt to bother the shooter. If the offensive player does a lot of faking with his shot off his dribble, the defensive player must dispense with the jumping. In *Diagram 4-20*, the defensive player allows the dribbler to move into the lane area and then attempts to block or harass the shot without fouling. To help this drill the shooter *must not fake the shot* so the defensive man gets the practice he needs in attempting to block the shot.

Diagram 4-20 also shows how to defense the shooter without fouling in the no-ball area. The player passes the ball to the offensive man and he tries to get a good shot. The defensive player should jump to block the shot only after the player has used his dribble or *after* he has jumped to shoot a jump shot. He must jump straight up, and not into the man with the arm

Diagram 4-20

closest to the shooter extended as high as possible. *It is better to have the defensive player concentrated more on making the player shoot a high arched shot, than on making an effort to block it.* When he tries to block the shot, he is more apt to foul by bringing his hand down into the arms of the shooter. He will block his share of shots if he extends his hand high enough, without the danger of fouling. *He should never drop away from his man in an attempt to make a clean block near the basket.* The danger of goal tending is too great with this move. When the player he is defensing does a lot of faking before shooting, the defensive player should keep his feet on the floor until the offensive player leaves his feet to take the shot.

In defensing the player off the ball, the players must keep part of their body between the ball and their man. When the offensive player tries to move toward the ball, the defensive player should force him backdoor with the body, *not* by using the hands and arms or extended legs and knees. By using the proper defensive movements with the feet and body along with the limited arm and hand action, you can play aggressive defense without fouling extensively.

Check Point No. 7

The last of the "check points" on defensive deals with the *offense*. A recovery by the opponents in this area will lead to a good shot almost everytime. A player cannot afford to make a careless pass when moving out of this area to go on the offensive.

There are a few fundamental rules that will keep your turnovers to a minimum in this area. They are (1) upon receiving a defensive rebound, turn first toward your basket before throwing the outlet pass; (2) upon receiving the outlet pass, turn first toward your basket before dribbling or passing; (3) never dribble in either situation—(1) or (2)—if a pass will get the same or better results in moving the ball out of the area; (4) if you do dribble in this area, do not stop your dribble until you have an open man to pass to; (5) whenever it is possible, move toward the outlet pass and not away from it.

SUMMARY

The offensive lane man-to-man defense is designed to do the following:

1. Pressure the player with the ball at all times in the lane area.
2. Prevent penetration into the no-ball area by a pass or dribble.
3. Push the offense out of the lane area.
4. Force the player cutting for the basket to go back door.
5. Slow up the well-executed offenses used against the man-to-man defense today.
6. Create turnovers, the prerequisite of any strong defense today.

In order to accomplish the above, it is necessary for the defensive player on the ball to:

1. Play with one hand high and be positioned two to three feet from his man.
2. Play his man tight if he has used his dribble.
3. After the pass by his man, move back one or two steps and in the direction of the pass.

The defensive players away from the ball must:

1. If "one pass away," use a preventive or closed stance.
2. If two or more passes away, use open stance and split the ball and the man.
3. Stay between the ball and man moving toward the basket and use a reverse pivot to open up when about to enter the foul lane area.
4. Front the man in the low post when the ball is in the C area.

5

A Zone That's Different

GENERAL DESCRIPTION OF ZONE

This zone defense has been designed to control the flow of the offensive pattern. This is done by attempting to make the offense follow the *line of least resistance*. When the offense falls into this pattern of movement, each defensive man should at least gain one step in covering the area for which he is responsible. It is only natural that a player's reaction to movement will be quicker if he has a preconceived idea of the path the ball is going to take. This should force the offense into taking more poor percentage shots. If the offense chooses to refuse to take the line of least resistance, this can also be beneficial to the defense. This means the offense is going to make a direct attack on the no-ball area. This area is most strongly defended by the defense and this choice could result in a greater number of turnovers by the offense, and usually does. The defensive alignment and duties in this zone are determined by the area the pass comes from and the area the pass goes into.

This type of coverage is used in most zone defenses. However, this zone differs from the conventional zones in the way the players move in and out of their areas of responsibility. When the player movement within the zone is correct, the area that one defensive player leaves will be covered immediately by another player. Much of the movement within this zone is the same as conventional zones, but when you begin to study the player's movements, you will see that it is a "zone that is different." *The movement within the zone has also been designed to fit within the multiple defense system, the Amoeba.* The movement of the guards helps in disguising the type of offensive lane defense that will be used.

   Close attention must be paid to the position of the body and feet in this zone. When the feet are in the proper position, the player is able to gain from one half to a full step in his movement to cover a certain area.

DEFENSIVE AREA

   It is common knowledge in basketball today that the only way you can cut down the efficiency of a good offensive basketball player is to apply pressure. If it is not applied, the skilled offensive player will score at will or make the pass that leads to an easy field goal. The defense is designed to harass the offensive player who has the ball, once he enters the 25-foot perimeter. If the chaser is not harrassing the player with the ball he is splitting the passing lane between the two guards. Which he does usually depends on the type of offense the opponents are using. The defense is also designed to prevent the ball from entering the 15-foot radius around the basket. When each man is moving properly, prevention can be accomplished to a degree that will definitely slow up the offense. Also, this defense would rather give a dribbler the baseline (four foot lane behind backboard) than have him penetrate the no-ball area. But when the dribbler is able to go baseline, he should be forced to stay in the four foot lane behind the backboard.

GENERAL POSITION, DESCRIPTION, AND DUTIES OF PLAYERS

   As the offense comes into the front court, *Diagram 5-1* indicates the general position of each defensive player. When he is able to do so, 1 will pick up the man with the ball as he comes over the center line. For the purpose of instruction and easy communication between coaches and players, each defensive position has a number. Players 1 and 2 are called the *chaser*.

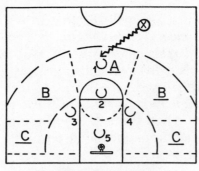

Diagram 5-1

They are usually the fastest and smallest players. In most cases, they would be the two offensive guards. Their main responsibilities are in the *A* and *B* areas. One or the other is constantly pressuring the man with the ball in these areas. Players 3 and 4 are called the *wingmen*. They are the biggest and strongest players. Their main responsibility is the lower *B* area and the no-ball area. Player 5 is called the *baseman*. Ideally, he is big and fast and has a "sixth sense" in diagnosing the offensive movement. He can become the quarterback of the defense. He must *talk* to the others when they tend to be out of position. His main responsibility is in the *C* area from sideline to sideline and in the no-ball area. The exceptions to these general rules will be noted as we go into each defensive alignment. This alignment is determined by: (1) the location of the ball; and (2) the area in which the ball is being dribbled or passed into. Usually the chasers will never go beyond the 25-foot perimeter after the initial penetration of the offense into the lane area. The wingmen *never* go beyond half way between foul line extended and the top of the foul circle extended in the *B* area. Whenever possible the 1 defensive player pressures the ball handler and attempts to force him to dribble to either right or left into the *B* area. He does not pressure him beyond the 25-foot imaginary line. He does not allow the dribbler to penetrate the no-ball area. Player 2 fronts the high postman if there is one. Players 3 and 4 must be stationed two to three feet below the foul line with the *right* foot and *left* foot on or near the line of the foul lane. Both wingmen should be anticipating a pass to the corner or foul lane area. If the two wingmen play their positions properly, it is very difficult for the ball handler to pass the ball into the no-ball area. They must keep their inside feet on or close to the first hash mark on the foul lane. Player 3 has his right foot forward, 4 has his left foot forward so that each one is facing the sidelines at a slight angle. Player 5 is in the foul lane area near the basket, "cheating" a little to the right or left if an offensive player is stationed in the low post area.

DEFENSIVE ALIGNMENT

A Area

The defense will attempt to keep the ball out of the A area, however, when the ball is located there the alignment of players is shown in *Diagram 5-1*.

If a pass is made from the A area into either corner, this can be a difficult coverage. If 3 and 4 are playing their position properly, each will be able to discourage this pass, because each is splitting the passing lane and the pass has to be a lob in order to get to the offensive man in either corner. If a lob is required to reach the player in the corner, either wingmen 3 or 4 going with the pass will be able to get to him and keep him from having an uncontested shot.

Pass from A to C Area

If the pass is successful to the corner, 1 must move fast to cover the stronside B area (*Diagram 5-2*); 3 must go with the pass and cover the player receiving the pass in the C area; 5

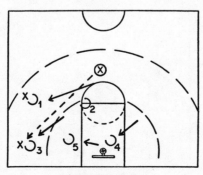

Diagram 5-2

must cover any player in the high or low post area. The defense always fronts the player in the low post position when the ball is in the *C* area. Player 2 will cover the area around the top of the key and foul line. He is always looking for the diagonal pass to *A* or weakside *B* area. If there is an offensive player in *both high and low post position*, he will cover the player in the high post and 5 will take care of the low post. Player 4 will protect the basket on the weak side and will move to the strong side when help is needed.

B Area

No. 1 must prevent an easy pass to the other offensive guard at the top of the foul circle and at the same time harass and push the dribbler into the double team with 3 in the 15- to 21-foot area or into passing to the corner; 2 fronts the high post man *(Diagram 5-3)*. If there is no high post man, he may "cheat" and attempt to create a turnover if the ball is lobbed carelessly back toward the *A* area. If the dribbler tries to penetrate the gap between 1 and 3, 3 moves out fast and forces him into double team with 1. The double team should force the pass to the man open in the corner or force a continued dribble toward the corner. Player 3 must stay with the dribbler until 5 picks him up or until the dribbler is forced to stop at the baseline. *Player 3 must give the six to nine foot lane (see Diagram 5-5)* to the corner and prevent any good pass into the no-ball area. Player 4 protects the basket on the weak side. He must *not* let the pass penetrate the foul lane area on the weak

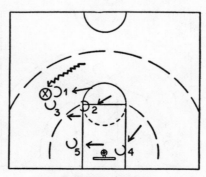

Diagram 5-3

side underneath the basket. He must *not* cross over to the strongside, unless the pass is on its way to the no-ball area on the strongside and it is evident help is needed. Player 5 protects the basket on the strongside. He must not let the pass penetrate the foul lane area underneath the basket on the strongside. He does *not* move toward the offensive player in the corner until the ball is passed from the B area toward the corner. He must *never* anticipate the pass to the corner in an attempt to intercept it.

Floor Area Responsibility When the Ball Is in B Area

From this double team, there are five general areas into which the ball handler may pass the ball. *Diagram 5-4* shows the area each defensive man is responsible for when the pass is made. The outside passing lane is left open for an easy pass into the corner. The defense alignment makes it more difficult to pass to the other areas and very difficult to pass into the no-ball area. The proper alignment of the players when double-teaming the player with the ball in the B area is necessary to make the defense more effective. Exact footwork and arm work are essential in this double team by 3 and 1. Player 2 fronts any offensive player in the high post area. Player 3's body position makes it difficult for a pass to enter the no-ball area. Player 5 protects the strong side and 4 protects the weak side of the no-ball area. If 1 and 3 do a good job in double teaming, 2 and 4 can cover the players that may receive the pass in other areas. It is almost impossible to "thread the needle" with a pass to the weakside C area.

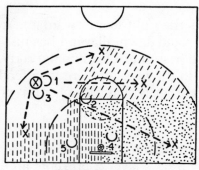

Diagram 5-4

Funneling the Ball to Corner

When the ball is in *B* area on either side, the strong-side wingmen always use the same defensive stance to funnel the ball to the corner *(Diagram 5-5)*. There are a number of good reasons for funneling the ball to the corner. (1) We can then force certain pass patterns. The defensive players cover their areas much better when this happens. (2) By giving these 6 to 9 foot lanes on each side we are able to concentrate our defense and better prevent the ball from getting into the no-ball area. (3) The corner shot is the poorest percentage shot for most players. It is also more difficult to have the shot bounce around and roll in (luck shot). (4) We can shut off passing lanes better when the ball is in the corner. (5) We can set up the double-team trap along the baseline. (6) A missed corner shot is ideal for a fast break situation. Your opponent's guards are often caught inside and there is a breakdown in their fastbreak defense.

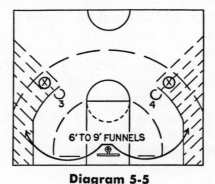

Diagram 5-5

Player 3 has the right foot forward and left foot back, right hand up and left hand down. Player 4 has just the opposite. This helps to force the pass or dribble into the corner. It also makes it easier to retreat to the area they are to defend when the ball is passed into the corner without losing sight of the ball.

C Area

Player 1 shuts off the passing lane for the return pass to the *B* area *(Diagram 5-6)*. Player 2 prevents an easy pass to offensive man in the *A* area or weakside *B* area. Player 3 shuts off the

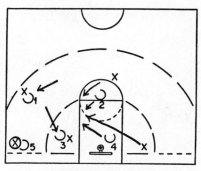

Diagram 5-6

passing lane to the offensive man in the post area. Player 4 protects the basket area, but remains on the weakside near the basket, unless the ball is passed into the no-ball area, and 3 defensive player needs help. When 4 is forced to move to the strongside he shouts "Drop" and 2, in the *A* area or weakside *B* area, drops back to protect the basket area on the weakside.

Player 2 plays the offensive man in the *A* or weakside *B* area on a *man-to-man basis,* if the offensive man cuts toward the strong side *C* through the foul lane area, he goes with him as far as the first hash mark on the foul lane on the strong side. Player 4 will do the same when the player comes from the weakside *C* into strongside. This *man-to-man defense to the strongside by 2 and 4 only takes place when the ball is in the corner and 3 is already guarding a man in the high or low post. If 3 is not guarding anyone, 4 warns 3* to pick up the offensive player moving over from the weakside by shouting "high" or "low." Player 3 must *open up* when he has no one to guard, so he may see on offensive player if he moves into the strongside high or medium post area from the weakside. He does this in much the same way as a defensive player does when guarding a weakside player in the man-to-man defense.

Pass From B to Strong-Side C Area

When the pass is made from the *B* area to the strong-side *C* area, 3 *must move with the pass* and front the man in the high or low post by the time the ball reaches the corner or at least a split second after the ball reaches there (*Diagram 5-7*). If there is an

Diagram 5-7

offensive man in both the high and low post, he must front the low postman and 2 will front the high post man. It is important that 2 use a closed stance with the *right* foot and extended right arm between the high post man and the ball as illustrated in *Diagram* 5-7. He must not be screened out by the high post man if he has to move to the weak side on a diagonal pass from the *C* area. If there is just one offensive player in the post area, he must front him. If there is neither a high nor low post man, 3 covers the medium post area in an *open-up position, halfway between the foul line and baseline,* ready to take any offensive player that may come into the area.

When the ball is passed from *B* to strong-side *C*, 5 moves with the pass to cover the man with the ball in the corner. He must make it very difficult for the offensive player to dribble into the no-ball area, even if he is forced to give him the baseline. If the player in the corner proves to be a "hot" shooter from this spot, 5 "cheats" toward him and tries to block his shot, leaving his feet if necessary. He does not worry about the offensive man's fake and drive; 3 is ready to pick him up; 5 *must not move toward the man in the corner* until the pass is on its way to the *C* area. Also, as 5 is moving toward him, he must always look for a pass to the high or low post and try to deflect it. If the player in the *C* area tries to make a quick pass to the low post, 5 usually is from six to twelve feet away from him although he may be moving fast. At that distance, if he is alert, he has a good chance to deflect the pass. In other words, *he is in a sense splitting the passing lane even though he is on the move.* Player 5 becomes much more valuable to the defense if he is always alert and ready for this pass into the low post from the corner. With this type of defense, 5 is giving 3 a better chance to cover his responsibilities in the low post area.

Pass From B to A Area

When the ball is passed from the *B* to *A* area *(Diagram 5-8)*, 1 must open to the ball and slide as quickly as possible back to the foul line to take 2's position. Player 1 must also make it as difficult as possible for the player to pass to *A* area. *Player number 2 should not leave his position when there is an offensive player in the high post, until 1 is within six feet* of replacing him. Player 2 can move with the pass, when there is no high post man. Numbers 3, 4, and 5 return to their regular positions when the ball is in the *A* area.

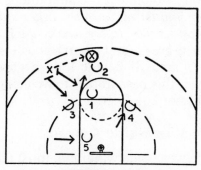

Diagram 5-8

Pass From B to Weak-side B Area

Since the ball is in the *B* area, the same responsibilities as in *Diagram 5-3* apply, only on the other side of the court. If the pass is in the lower part of the weak-side *B* area 4 must cover the player receiving the ball until 2 can release the high postman (if there is one) to 1 *(Diagram 5-9)*. As soon as 1 is about to enter the foul circle, 2 may release and help 4 by double-teaming with him. Player 2 may decide it is better to split the passing lane of the guards rather than double-team with 4. He uses this option when the opponent is successful in reversing the ball. This is

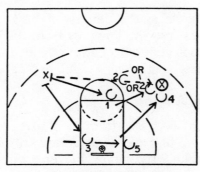

Diagram 5-9

also the best thing to do if the guards are passing back and forth
to each other a number of times. Player 4 should be ready to
intercept if the pass is lazy, weak or not accurate. However, he
should not leave his proper position until the pass is on its way.
Player 4's first job is to protect the area under the basket on the
weak side. *Player 5 must move to the other side of the foul lane
when the pass is on its way to the weak-side B area.* He must be
ready to cover the C area if and when the ball is passed from B to
the strong-side C area. If 3 and 1 do a good job on double-
teaming the player, this pass from B to weak-side B, is difficult to
make and should not be effective.

Pass From B to Weak-side C Area

Player 4, the weak-side wingman, must take the man in the
corner on this pass and should always be ready for a possible
interception, if it is carelessly executed (*Diagram 5-10*). 4 is in a
much better position to cover the pass in the weak-side corner
than 5. Player 5 will take care of the foul lane area guarding the
man in the high or low post. Numbers 2, 3, and 4 take care of
the areas shown on diagram. They have the same responsibilities as described in detail on diagrams 6 and 7. Whoever is
guarding the man with the ball in the corner must go with him if
he dribbles from the corner toward the backcourt. He will stay
with the dribbler until 1 or 2 picks him up (*in this diagram, 2*).
Player 4 then could double-team the dribbler with 2, if the dribbler stops when 2 picks him up. If 2 does not stop the dribbler

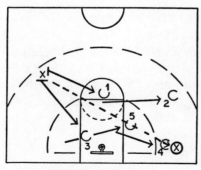

Diagram 5-10

and he continues toward the back court, 4 should then return to his proper position.

REBOUND ALIGNMENTS

Shot From C Area

When the ball is shot from the corner (C area) and missed, one of the better opportunities for the fast break appears. If our players are doing a good job on the defensive board in rebounding, 5, after harassing the shooter, will lead the fastbreak (*Diagram 5-11*). If the team is having trouble on the boards, he will help on the long rebound to the strong side. Player 1 will block out the offensive man in his area and also help on the long rebound strong side. Player 2 must block out the high postman

Diagram 5-11

(if there is one) and get the long rebound down the center or to the weak side. This *block out is important.* A good big man will come in from the high post and get the offensive rebound if he is not blocked. Numbers 3 and 4 will take care of the short rebound on each side and the front of the basket. If the pass is made from the *C* area to the no-ball area, and then the shot is taken, the rebound alignment is the same.

Shot From A or B Area

The best rebound man, when possible, plays the 4 spot because more offenses move to their right and usually more shots are taken from the offensive right side of the court. This gives the best rebounder more opportunities to be in a good position for more rebounds. Therefore, with any shot taken on the offensive right in the *B* area and most of the *A* area, our rebound alignment is as shown in *Diagram 5-12.* Player 1 should be looking for fastbreak possibilities. Player 2 has the block out assignment for the player coming from the high post area. Players 4 and 5 have short rebound responsibility. If the pass is made from this *A* or *B* area *into* the no-ball area and a shot is taken, rebounding responsibilities are the same. When a shot is taken from the *B* area on the offensive left, our rebound alignment is as follows: 1 looks for a possible fastbreak; 2 will still block out the player at the high post, then take the long rebound on his side. Players 3 and 5 have short rebound responsibility. Player 4, because of his position away from the basket

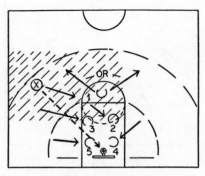

Diagram 5-12

when the ball is located in *B* area on his side of the floor, must take care of the long rebound.

BASELINE DOUBLE TEAM TRAP

Since this zone normally has 1 cutting off the pass from the *C* area to strongside *B*, 1 is not able to help 5 if the offensive player in the corner with the ball decides to drive on him away from the baseline. To prevent an easy drive into the no-ball area, 5 plays the driver slightly away from the baseline. This is done even at the expense of giving the driver the baseline. *Due to the nature of our zone movement, giving the baseline (normally considered a weakness in defense) can become a strength.*

When the driver goes baseline, 5 must keep the dribbler in the four foot lane between the baseline and backboard. The other four defensive men must *always* be alert for this baseline drive and must move to their proper positions as soon as he starts his drive. Player 3 cuts off the baseline and double-teams the dribbler with 5. It is easier for 3 to do this than it seems. He is usually moving toward the baseline when the offensive man begins his drive (often before he begins it). This makes it much easier for him to be in position to stop the drive and double-team with 5. Players 1, 2 and 4 umbrella the strong side and around the basket, ready to intercept the outlet pass. This has been a very successful movement in this defense for the last sixteen years (*Diagram 5-13*). The term "umbrella" will be explained in the next chapter.

Diagram 5-13

Diagram 5-14

When an offensive player proves to be a good shot from the corner, 5 will attempt to harass or block the shot by jumping high. If the offensive player fakes and drives the baseline, we still may have the double team trap and umbrella (*Diagram 5-14*).

DEFENSIVE ALIGNMENT WITH BALL OUT-OF-BOUNDS

The defense is usually most vulnerable in this situation (*Diagram 5-15*). The offense can set up a play inside the three-second area of the foul lane. Regardless of what defense is being used when the ball goes out-of-bounds under the opponent's basket, we always play *zone* on any inbound pass. When the ball is taken out on the right of the foul lane, the players line up as illustrated. Player 5 (baseman) takes the man with the ball, right hand up facing strong side. *Facing the strong side is very im-*

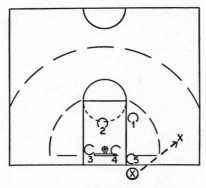

Diagram 5-15

portant, because covering the no-ball area is much easier and 5 can go to the strong side corner faster. Player 4 protects the basket while facing the strong side. He is ready for the lob to the big man in the foul lane. Player 3 does the same, facing the strong side, but protecting the weak side of the basket area. Players 1 and 2 protect the high post area, both leaning toward the strong side. Player 2 is in position to "free-lance" or gamble on this defensive setup. When 3 and 4 play their position correctly, with the help of the backboard, the passing lane into 2's area is completely blocked off. This gives 2 the opportunity to be alert for a careless lob to the back court by the out-of-bounds passer.

It is very difficult to pass into the no-ball area with the concentration of all five defensive players in the foul lane area. Player 5 tries to make it easy to pass to the offensive player in the strong side corner. When the pass is made, 5, ready for this pass, moves quickly with the pass and should prevent an uncontested shot from the corner.

Conventional Move

In *Diagram 5-16,* 2 makes the conventional move in the zone. This makes the defensive alignment the same as in *Diagrams 7* and *8* with the ball located in the C area.

If you position your defensive players properly, it makes penetration by the pass from the out-of-bounds into the no-ball area very difficult. Player 4 is responsible for a high lob near the basket. He should always be ready for this pass when a big man is stationed there.

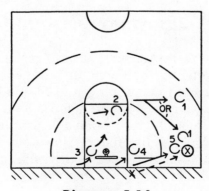

Diagram 5-16

This defensive alignment has been very successful. The opponents seldom get an easy lay-up and the defense has created numerous turnovers. We had so much confidence in this defensive alignment that our defensive rebounders were instructed to knock the ball out-of-bounds, if they were unable to get both hands on a rebound.

Player 3 should use movements to discourage a pass being made to the weak-side corner. If the out-of-bounds player moves back from the line, this means he want to pass to the weak-side corner. Player 3 should be ready for this and move with the pass to prevent the offensive man in the weak-side corner from getting an easy shot. If the ball is passed to the weak-side corner, the defense alignment finds 3 on the ball, 4 protecting the low post area, and 5 protecting the weak-side basket area. Players 2 and 1 protect the *B* and *A* area respectively.

Double Teaming

The double team in the corner on the inbound pass has been a very successful move option of 1 in *Diagram 5-16*. It is always a good time to double-team when the player receiving the ball is not tall. This happens quite frequently because the player receiving the ball is often the opponent's offensive guard. Player 1 will double-team with 5 in the corner and players 2, 4, and 3 will form a tight umbrella on the strong side.

If the offensive man takes the ball on the left side of the foul lane, 5 is on the ball, 3 is in low post area and 4 is in weak-side low post area. *Player 5 is always on the ball* regardless of the side of the foul lane used to take the ball out.

ADJUSTING THE ZONE

There are times when you have to make a major adjustment in your defense alignment in order to prevent a well-planned offense from penetrating into the no-ball area. Every defense has its weakness, and this defense is no exception. Most zone defenses can be effective when able to adjust and cover up a weakness the offense has found. However, any adjustments that are necessary should be learned on the practice floor and not in the middle of a tough game. You can only have this necessary flexibility in your zone if you have prepared for it in advance. *The secret of a strong zone defense is its adjustability.*

In our zone, if the offensive player in the C area is driving with ease into the no-ball area, or if he is beating the double team on the baseline, an adjustment must be made. The change necessary in this situation involves only 5 (baseman) and 1 (chaser). Player 1 merely drops into the no-ball area of the strongside B instead of attempting to cut off the pass to the player in the offensive lane. Player 5 adjusts his defensive position by playing the man with the ball in the C area head on. Now the dribbler should have a more difficult time driving baseline. If he drives away from the baseline, 1 in his new position can assist in stopping the drive into the no-ball area. This adjustment is also necessary if the player in the C area is having too much success passing the ball into the high or medium post area (*Diagram 5-17*).

This change will work well until an alert opponent realizes what has been done. The defense has now become vulnerable to a weakness which is common to most conventional zone defenses. A quick reversal by passing the ball back to the weakside can be made because 1 is not cutting off the passing lane back to the strong side B. Then a pass can be made quickly from C to strong side B, then to A or weakside B before the defense can adjust, and the offense will get an uncontested fifteen to eighteen foot jump shot. This type of attack may be slowed considerably however, if 1 recovers quickly and makes it difficult for the player in B area to make the quick pass to the weak side by

Diagram 5-17

Diagram 5-18

playing him strong away from the sideline. At the same time, 2 must split the passing lane from the strong side *C* to *A* or to the weak side *B* area by making the long diagonal pass to those areas difficult. *Player 2 must be careful not to drop too deeply into the no-ball area and thus leave this passing lane open (Diagram 5-18).*

Another offensive maneuver that may be successful against this zone is to have the two guards play with the ball by passing back and forth in the *A* and *B* areas. This would eventually have our chasers running in circles. To counteract this, we have 1 wait until after the third or fourth pass, and then split the passing lane by playing about two-thirds of the distance away from the guard with the ball. This will force the offense to move into the zone or toward the sideline and corner. When 1 does split the passing lane, the 3 or 4 wingman must close the gap to prevent penetration by dribble or pass into the no-ball area *(Diagram 5-19).*

Another adjustment is necessary when the offense has a player who is shooting well from the corners. This is a shot we usually allow (especially from the deep corner). Player 5 should always try to at least hurry the shot. However, when a certain player proves to be able to make a high percentage from the corner, 5 will "cheat" toward this corner and attempt to force him to drive or pass off. Player 5 is instructed to leave his feet to bother the shot, if necessary. If the player fakes his shot and drives, there is back-up help. When 5 is forced to jump in an attempt to block the shot, he jumps to the left of the shooter,

Diagram 5-19

forcing the base line drive if the player fakes the shot. Players 4 and 2, seeing 5 jump, will move as indicated in *Diagram 5-14*. Player 4 helps 3 on the double team and players 1, 2, and 5 umbrella. Player 5 has the liberty to move toward our basket for a fast break if he feels he is too far out of play to help by coming back.

DRILLS ON ZONE

The following drills help teach the defensive player his position. These drills give each player confidence in his ability to cover the floor area of his responsibility.

Chasers

Pass the ball back and forth from *A* area to *B* area. Do not pass too fast. This drill is to help the 1 and 2 men to learn the proper foot work and position when the ball is passed from the *A* to *B* area (*Diagram 5-20*). Timing is important in this drill. It is the job of the 2 man to front the offensive player in the high post or the foul line area. When a pass goes from the *B* to the *A* area, 2 must not quit fronting the man in the high post until 1 has replaced him. This means that when the ball is passed from *B* to *A* area, if there is an offensive player in the high position, 2 must hold his position until 1 is at least within six to nine feet from the high post before 2 moves out to the player with the ball in the *A* area. The greater the distance 1 is from the high post area in covering the man with the ball in the *B* area, the longer 2 must

Diagram 5-20

wait before covering the player who received the ball in the *A* area.

Wingman and Baseman

The ball is passed from the *B* area to the strong side *C* area and then to the low post. This drill will determine the range each wingman has. Some players are able to come out on the man with the ball in *B* area to within *several feet* of an imaginary line extended from the top of the foul circle (see line in *Diagram 5-21*). It depends on their quickness. The slower, less agile player will not be able to come out that far; however, a wingman must be able to come out at least beyond the foul line extended to make the defense effective.

When the ball is passed from the coach to X^2, 3 must be able to get back and front the offensive player in the low post area, before the player in *C* area can pass the ball to the low post

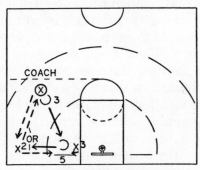

Diagram 5-21

position X^3. Player 5 moves over to cover X^2, making it difficult for him to pass to the low post. Player 5 makes the pass difficult by being alert for the quick pass while moving toward X^2. Even though he is moving, he will in a sense be splitting the passing lane. This helps give 3 the necessary time to defend the low post area. When X^2 does not feel he is able to pass to X^3 successfully, he should pass the ball back to the coach. The coach waits until the defensive players move back to their proper positions. The drill is then repeated. This drill helps each wingman find his own range. The wingman *must* be able to cover the low post if the defense is to be successful.

Chaser, Wingman, and Baseman

This drill is practiced against the *overload* by the offense, using four defensive men against the coach and four offense players (*Diagram* 5-22). The offensive players can move the ball anywhere they desire on *one side of the court only*. They must not move the ball to the other side.

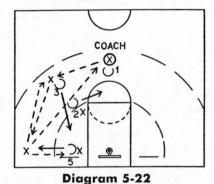

Diagram 5-22

No-Ball

This drill will give you a good insight on how well the players know their responsibilities in this defense. A coach stands in *A* area, three or four feet beyond the top of the circle in the foul lane area and calls out the movement of the ball. Example: *A* to right *C* (players right)—players move to their proper positions. Other examples: *C* to strong side *B; B* to weak side *C; C* to *A; A* to left *B; B* to *A; A* to left *C; C* to weak side *B; B* to no-ball area, etc. If your players know their position, they only need a second or two before responding to each command. The coach should wait two or three more seconds between each command. A player that gets mixed up too often does not know the defense well enough and needs more work on it.

Double Team

This drill helps to perfect the double team on the baseline. A player drives from *C* area on the baseline toward the basket (*Diagram* 5-23). Player 5 keeps forcing him into the lane behind the backboard. Player 3 (wingman) coming back to cover the low post double teams with 5. The coach stands out near the foul line. Players 3 and 5 attempt to prevent the driver from passing the ball to him. The coach may also move in toward the basket to receive the pass.

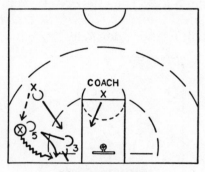

Diagram 5-23

Six Man

This drill gives our defense a good workout, using six men on offense and letting them move anywhere they want. Everybody must really move to keep the offense from getting good shots. However, if the players move to their positions properly, they can keep the ball out of the no-ball area much of the time.

SUMMARY

This zone defense is designed to do the following:

1. Pressure the offensive guards up to 25 feet from the basket.
2. Prevent penetration into the no-ball area by a pass or dribble.

3. Force the offense to pass or dribble into the corner or near the corner.
4. Cut off the passing lanes when the ball is located in the corner or near the corner.
5. Double-team the offensive man with the ball in *B* area when he is in the good shooting percentage area (21 feet or closer).
6. Double-team the offensive player when he attempts to drive the baseline.
7. Cut off all short passes when possible and force the long pass.
8. Slow up the well-executed offenses used against the zone today.
9. Create turnovers, the prerequisite of any strong defense today.

In order to accomplish these goals the 1 defensive player picks up the player with the ball when he crosses the center line whenever possible. Once the offense has entered the offensive lane, the defense must pressure the ball at all times. The defense must force the offense to move along the line of least resistance and at the same time cut off all passing lanes to the no-ball area.

6

Half-Court Man-to-Man and Zone Pressure Defense with Jump-Switch

PRIMARY GOAL OF DEFENSE

The primary goal of the Amoeba defense is to apply pressure on the ball from one end of the court to the other. This, of course, is not always possible after a missed field goal or foul shot or when the offense has a turnover. Even when these conditions take place, the defense attempts to pick up the man with the ball before or as he crosses the center line. There are times, of course, that for various reasons the defense will drop back to the offensive lane before picking up the man with the ball. There are also times when the defense will fall back into a half court pressure defense. When in this defense, the 1 defensive player must try to meet the player with the ball as he crosses the center line. Whenever it is possible, the defensive players off the ball must also get to their man before he crosses the line. I have found that this is not an unreasonable request when the opponents are not able to throw the long pass. An alert defense is able to prevent the successful long pass most of the time. When the defense is able to meet the offense at the center line, the chance of forcing them out of their planned offensive attack is much better.

In the half-court pressure defense, the A area is extended out to the center line (Diagram 6-1). The player with the ball must be pushed out of or across this area. The dribbler must not penetrate into the lane and the no-ball area through this 12-foot

138

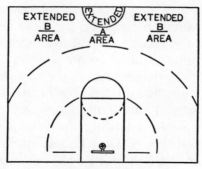

Diagram 6-1

alley. The defense must force the dribbler toward the sidelines and into the extended *B* area.

Before I go into the details of explaining this half-court pressure defense, I will discuss the *jump-switch,* which is very important in all the defensive tactics. Some coaches call this move the "run and jump." When starting to use the defensive move back in 1965–66 I called it the "jump-switch" because it best expresses what actually takes place. The length of the switch in the defense depends, in most cases, on the distance the player with the ball is away from his basket. It may be as many as 24 feet or it may be only a few feet. When pressing full court, the switch may be rather long, but when in the half-court press it is seldom more than 12 to 18 feet. In the offensive lane area it should only be from 6 to 12 feet.

The jump-switch revolutionized my whole thinking on defense. This defensive move became the cornerstone to our overall defensive strategy. It has been the key that has made the combination or multiple defense called the "Amoeba" possible. By combining this move along with both zone and man-to-man defensive principles, we exerted a defense that could confuse the most sophisticated offense.

PROPER EXECUTION OF THE JUMP-SWITCH

Although the footwork is basic and not difficult, I have found that some players have trouble executing it properly. This is due to being timid about moving head-on in front of a dribbler who may be moving at a good rate of speed. But when the jump-switch is executed properly, the defensive player can absorb the shock of the charge with little chance of physical harm. The number of steps required before the jump may be only one or can be five or six, depending on the distance the dribbler is away when the move is initiated. When the jump is made, the feet should be spread the same distance required in a good defensive stance when guarding the man with the ball. Just before the jump he shouts "Go." This is important, because the defensive man on the ball will be able to complete the switch faster. At completion of the jump, both feet should hit the floor at the same time, parallel to each other. The feet should come down about three feet in front of the dribbler. This distance could be a little less or more, depending on the speed of the dribbler. Hands should be just above the shoulders, in a spread position. As the feet hit the floor, the player should be at a complete stop with his weight placed lightly on the heels. This is done for two reasons. If the dribbler collides with the defensive player, he is able to go with the dribbler and the contact is minimized. Second, if the dribbler keeps going, but avoids contact, the defensive player can stay with him. He must be ready to reverse his direction, and if his body weight is on the front part of his feet at the completion of the jump, it makes changing direction more difficult.

The defensive player should not *fake* the contact, looking for the charge call. This is not necessary, and besides it only gives the officials a good reason to ignore the legitimate charge. Players should be instructed to wait until contact is made and then go with the dribbler. They should *not* fall flat on their backs on the floor if they can avoid it. They should try to stay on their feet, after contact, whenever it is possible. The number 2 defensive player always initiates the jump-switch. He determines when the move should be made. There are certain rules he must follow (see page 185).

DEFENSIVE PLAYERS NUMBERED

In the jump-switch pressure defense the players are numbered from 1 to 5. These numbers are very important in this defense. Player 1 *always* guards the man with the ball. Player 2 is *always* the player who initiates the jump-switch. If three or more players are involved, either 3 or 4 will take 2's man when he makes the jump-switch. Player 5 is *always* the man who protects the basket area.

It is possible that *any player* can be 1, 2, 3, 4 or 5 at one time or another during the course of a game. The number of defensive players involved *depends on what 2's man does when 2 makes his jump-switch.* If he does not move, or is slow in making his move, only 1 and 2 are involved. If he moves with any kind of speed toward the baseline or his basket, 3, 4, or 5 may be involved. When more than two players are involved in the movement, it resembles a *chain reaction.* Player 2 takes 1's man; 3 takes 2's man; 5 takes 3's man, etc. The strong-side defensive players *usually are moving toward the ball* and the weak-side defensive man, in *most cases, will be moving toward the opponent's basket.* The offensive man that 1 ends up guarding depends on the number of players involved in the rotation. If all five players are involved, he could end up by taking the guard on the weak side.

The numbering of players in this matter is confusing at first. However, I found that in teaching the defense, it was imperative to number the players in accordance with the responsibility they had. When instructing them, it was much easier to say "you were 2 in this situation." Once they mastered the duties of all five positions in relation to the numbers, the understanding of what we were trying to accomplish became much clearer to them. *This will also be true with the reader of this book.* Another good reason for the number system is that it is easier for the players to operate efficiently when all they have to say is "I'll take five" or "you take five," etc. Talking is important in playing good defense.

DRILLS ON THE JUMP-SWITCH

Diagram 6-2 illustrates a drill which gives the players practice in executing the jump-switch properly. The player guarded by 1 dribbles, and 2 makes the jump-switch. Player 1 moves down the floor, 2 forces the dribbler toward 1 and then 1 jump-switches. This continues the length of the floor. To give the player the proper practice the dribbler stops (*but keeps his drib-*

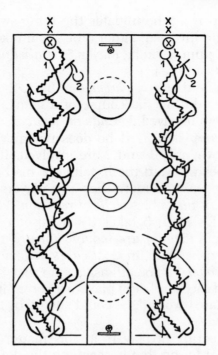

Diagram 6-2

ble) when the jump-switch is made. He then changes direction with his dribble. At the center court and at the completion at the end of the court, they also practice the double team move. *Player 1 always determines when the double team takes place.* Player 2 also gets practice in saying "Go" when he makes the switch.

Diagram 6-3 is a drill which gives the player practice on the chain reaction move that involves three or more players. The coach dribbles and 2 makes the jump-switch; 3 takes 2's man; 5 takes 3's man; 4 takes 5's man; and 1 takes 4's man. If 5 does not take 3's man, then 1 must take him and only three players are involved. If 4 does not take 5's man, then only four players are involved. Player 2's man is the only offensive player to move in this drill. He moves toward the baseline as indicated in the diagram. When he does *not move* or *moves toward backcourt* only two defensive players are involved. In this drill 2's man should mix up all three—forward, backward and stand still. This helps the defense to learn how many players should be involved

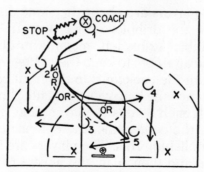

Diagram 6-3

in its *chain reaction*, which is determined by what 2's man does. The arrow shows the different players 1 takes, depending on the number of switches involved. At the completion of the moves, the coach dribbles back to the center line, 2, who is now 1, going with him. He then starts the dribble toward the new 2 player. Each player gets practice in every position. The coach just keeps dribbling back and forth and the drill continues. You may also run this drill starting deep into the back-court.

THE JUMP-SWITCH WITH TWO PLAYERS INVOLVED

In *Diagram 6-4*, the offensive player with the ball in the backcourt is approaching the extended *A* area. The defensive player is ready to force him toward either of the *B* areas. Which way he forces him, in most cases, depends on where the next closest defensive man is located. In this particular case, both 2

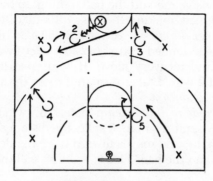

Diagram 6-4

and 3 defensive players are about the same distance from him, so he may force the dribbler either way. In *Diagram 6-4* he defenses the dribbler to his left, moving him toward 2.

The defense attempts to keep their opponents from making the *long* pass from the backcourt to the front court. They would like them to advance the ball over the center line using a dribble or a short pass. If each defensive player picks up his man before or as he crosses the center line, the defense can often be successful in accomplishing this. The players are instructed to play between the ball and their man and always *be prepared* for the long pass. How far a defender "splits" his man depends on the distance he is away from the ball. If the offense dribbles across the center line into the front court, the defense wants to use the jump-switch as soon as possible. *What 2's man does when 2 makes his jump-switch has much to do with the defensive movement.*

In *Diagram 6-4*, 2's man moves very little or away from the basket, when 2 makes his jump-switch. Under these circumstances, there will just be a two-man switch. *On all jump-switches*, 2 shouts *"Go"* just before he makes his jump; 1 already is moving toward 2's man, *picks up speed* (important) on hearing 2's command and the switch is made quickly. *1 should always be alert for this signal to GO.* The success of the switch is dependent on how much time it takes for him to get to 2's man. What takes place now depends partly on *what the player with the ball does and what the number 1 defensive player decides to do.*

1. If he stops his dribble, 2 moves up close with arms flaring. The defensive men off the ball tighten up their defense with a closed stance, making the pass difficult (*Diagram 6-4*).
2. If a dribbler *changes directions*, 3 will stop his attempt to drive down the extended *A* area (12-foot alley) with a jump-switch or help and recovery move. If 3 jump-switches, 5 takes 3's man and 2 would take 5's man if more than two players were involved (*Diagram 6-5*).
3. *1 may decide to double team* instead of switching. If he does, 4 moves closer to 2's man, 5 splits the distance between his man and 4's man; and moves toward the extended *A* area between his man and the ball. This is what we call the "umbrella." It is

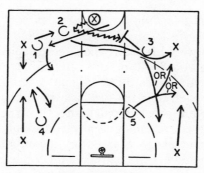

Diagram 6-5

the term used for the positioning of the three defensive players not in the "double team." They surround the double team in a way that resembles the shape of an open umbrella. The umbrella is used in all the different defenses when we double-team. The size of the umbrella is determined by the distance the double team is away from the opponent's basket. The farther the double team is from the basket, the larger the umbrella. When a dribbler experiences success in changing direction on the jump-switch, he often charges right into 1, when 1 decided to stay and double-team rather than moving on down court to take the open offensive player. After the dribbler has one experience like this, he is never sure that he will be successful if he changes directions again on the jump-switch. Mixing the jump-switch with the double team keeps the dribbler guessing. *His mind is now on what the defense will do and not on getting the offense started* (Diagram 6-6).

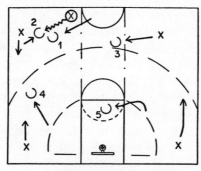

Diagram 6-6

4. *The dribbler looking for jump-switch does not move forward, but maintains his dribble. Player 2 should fake* a jump-switch and stay with his man when the dribbler does this. A good offensive guard will do this after he has been fooled by the switch a few times. Player 2 may fake a switch two or three times or each time the dribbler starts moving forward again. The fake jump-switch will bother this type of offensive guard. When he is cautious and always looking for this switch, he will not do a good job in getting the offense started. He has a tendency to hold the ball too long, while waiting to see what the defense is going to do. The *fake* jump-switch has become a very important part of this whole defensive system.

The main strategy in using these defensive maneuvers is to upset the opponent's 1 guard (the quarterback of the offense). When he starts thinking about what the defense is doing, he tends to forget about his job of running the offense. The defense is then able to keep the opponents out of their planned offensive pattern. This often results in a greater number of recoveries. Most recoveries in this defense are the result of a *team* effort (two or more players) rather than of one man alone.

JUMP-SWITCH WITH THREE OR MORE PLAYERS INVOLVED

Diagrams 6-7 to 6-10 illustrate the various options when 2's man makes a *definite* move toward another defensive man or in the general direction of the offensive basket, after the jump-switch is made. It is very important that all the players off the ball *watch to see what 2's man does* after 2 makes the jump-switch. What he does determines their move and the quicker they make it, the more effective the defense is. *Diagram 6-7* shows the approximate distance each of the defensive players move when they see 2 make the jump-switch and 2's man moving in the direction of the 4 defensive player. It is important that all other defensive men move into a ready position when they see 2 starting his jump-switch. This extra step or two gives the defense a better chance to involve other defensive players in the move if the opportunity is available.

Diagram 6-8 shows defensive moves when three men are involved in the switch; 2 takes 1's man; 4 takes 2's man; and 1

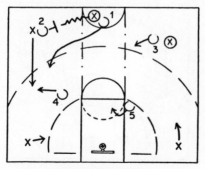

Diagram 6-7

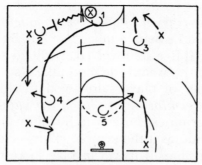

Diagram 6-8

takes 4's man. When Coach Ridl and I first started to do this fifteen years ago, we were worried about the *mismatch* (our 6' guard having to defense a 6'9" center). However, we found that we were seldom hurt. We did take the necessary precautions to keep this weakness at a minimum by having our small guard front the big man and instructed our weak-side defensive man (third man on defense) to be always ready to help on the lob. We always wanted to have what we call the *"third man on defense"* ready to help on any defensive switch made. This was especially true when there was a mismatch. The players were instructed to be alert for the mismatch and to get the small guard back to defensing his own man as soon as possible.

Diagram 6-9 illustrates the movement when four or five defensive players are involved. The involvement of more than three players only takes place when the offensive players are in an ideal position for it. *It may take place only three or four times*

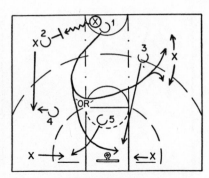

Diagram 6-9

*during a game or as high as twenty or more times. This will
depend upon the type of offense the opponents use.* If four are
involved—2 takes 1's man; 4 takes 2's man; 5 takes 4's man; and
1 takes 5's man. If five are involved, 3 will take 5's man and thus
1 must move to the weak side, and take 3's man.

The number of players involved in this chain reaction
movement is *determined entirely by the players.* In this given
situation, 4 determines if the switch will involve more than two
players; 5 determines if the switch will involve more than three
players; 3 determines if it will involve more than four players.
Player 1 must find the unguarded offensive player as he is moving back toward the opponent's basket. The chain reaction may
involve all five players. But, if at any point in the reaction, the
no-ball area is left unprotected in order to carry out the switch,
the reaction should stop. In *Diagram 6-8*, 5 did not feel it was
safe, so he did not make the switch and only three players were
involved.

In *Diagram 6-9*, 5 thought it was definitely safe to switch
so he took 4's man. He felt that 1 or 3 could take his man. I have
shown the path that 1 takes when there are both four and five
players involved. If only four players are involved, he takes 5's
man; if there are five players involved, 1 makes a half-circle
move and picks up 3's man. The arrows show either path that 1
may take.

In *Diagram 6-10*, 2's man moves toward 3 on the weak
side. Player 3 decides to take him. If 3's man does not move or
moves away from the basket, there will only be three players
involved, and 1 takes 3's man. However, if 3's man moves to-

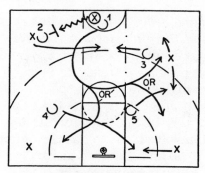

Diagram 6-10

ward the basket, or the baseline, four or five players may get involved. The diagram shows the path of 1 on each different possibility. Player 1 may take 4's man; or 5's man, as arrows indicate on the diagram.

Diagram 6-11 illustrates the possible three, four or five player involvement when 2's man moves toward the weakside 4. Player 1's path is shown in all three situations.

The main thing to remember is that players 3, 4 and 5 only get involved in this rotation movement if one of the offensive men left open by the jump-switch is moving toward one of the three and it would be a natural and easy move for him to take the open man. The only time he cannot *afford* to be a part of the rotation is when he happens to be in the 5 position. Player 5 only makes this move when he *knows* a teammate is on his way toward the basket and close enough to protect the area he is leaving. *It is safe to say that over 60 percent of the time during*

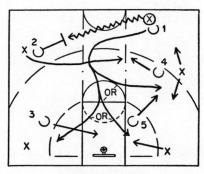

Diagram 6-11

the course of a game, when a jump-switch takes place between the center line and the offensive lane only two players are involved. Even when 2's man does move toward 3 or 4, they often are not in a good position or ready to take 2's man; therefore, there is just a two man switch. *Three players are involved possibly 20 to 30 percent of the time,* more than three players as little as three or four times during the game. It does not matter how many players are involved, as long as the defense accomplishes what it is trying to do and that is to disrupt the smooth penetration of the offense into the offensive lane. Of course, the desired goal is to create a turnover which it often does.

DOUBLE TEAM NEAR SIDELINE

If the man with the ball crosses the centerline and is dribbling near the out-of-bounds line as in *Diagram 6-12*, this is an ideal position to use the double team on the jump-switch. Players 3, 4 and 5 know that 1 may stay and double team so they are ready to "umbrella" as shown in diagram. If the pass is successful out of the double team, 1 must move fast to guard the open man if the *key* being used for playing in the offensive lane designates their still playing man-to-man. Player 4 would protect the basket area (*Diagram 6-13*). However the *double team may have keyed that the defense would be zone* after a successful pass out of the double team in this area. If this was the case, the whole team would fall back into a zone.

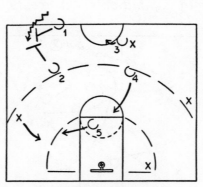

Diagram 6-12

KEYS DETERMINING DEFENSE

This is the first time I have mentioned the keys used in determining the type of defense that would be played when the offense entered the offensive lane. In *Diagram 6-13* the defense remains in man-to-man and continue to use pressure and could possibly get another jump-switch or double team before the offense is able to set up in the offensive lane.

In *Diagram 6-14*, the double team (must have player with ball trapped) keyed players that on successful pass out of it the defense would fall back into a zone. This is just one of the many keys that can be used in changing the defense during the course of action in the game. For example, in this series of events, the offense, while attacking the zone had a pass knocked out-of-

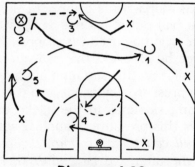

Diagram 6-13

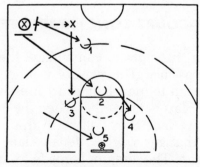

Diagram 6-14

bounds to the right of the defense. A pass coming inbounds from the right sidelines of the defense may key the defense to go back to their man-to-man. This constant changing of defense can completely disrupt the offense. One thing for certain, when the changes are executed properly, it definitely slows up the offensive attack.

OUT-OF-BOUNDS ON THE SIDE IN FRONT COURT

I have already explained that this defense always uses a zone when the ball is taken out under the opponent's basket in Chapter 5. However, when the ball is out-of-bounds on either side in the front court the pressure type man-to-man defense is always used. All in-bound passes will be pressured in an attempt to make it difficult for opponents to set up in the offensive lane. The players defense the in-bound pass in the same manner as when a player has stopped his dribble in the front court. The player taking the ball out-of-bounds is restricted in the same way as the player who has used his dribble. He must pass the ball from the spot he received the ball out-of-bounds. Proper execution of over-play on this situation often creates a *turnover*. This man-to-man pressure defense is also used when the ball is out-of-bounds along sidelines in the backcourt. The details of the different ways this pressure is applied will be explained in the chapter on *full court man-to-man defense*. What defense will be used in the offensive lane after the opponents break through this pressure will be determined by what *keys* are being used.

HALF-COURT ZONE (TRAP) DEFENSE

The defense attempts to camouflage the half court zone trap whenever possible. The players will set up in the same manner as our man-to-man half court pressure defense *(Diagram 6-15)*. The players know that when the offense finally sets up in the offensive lane they will be in the zone defense. The same principles that govern the offensive lane zone are used in this half court trap. The attempt is made to make it difficult to pass into the heart of the defense and make it relatively easy to

Diagram 6-15

pass or dribble down the side-line. If they do take the easy sideline route an attempt is made to double team in the general positions shown in *Diagrams 6-16, 6-17, and 6-18*, the three defensive players in the umbrella position attempt to pick off any pass in the direction of the no-ball area or across to the weak side. When the pass is eventually made toward the backcourt,

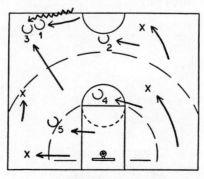

Diagram 6-16

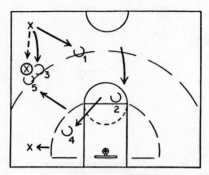

Diagram 6-17

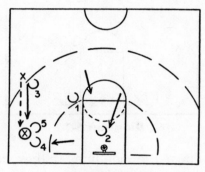

Diagram 6-18

the players move into the offensive lane *zone* as shown in *Diagram 6-19*.

Another difference in this half-court zone press from any other is that the jump-switch is used at times. The two chasers

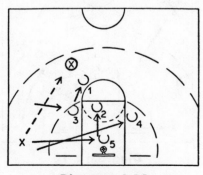

Diagram 6-19

in the zone—1 and 2—should *never double-team together* in this defense. They will use the jump-switch, however, if the dribbler is moving toward them or attempting to penetrate into the heart of the defense. In *Diagram 6-20* the guard is dribbling toward 2 as he crosses the centerline. Player 2 makes the jump-switch and 1 continues to move to his zone position. The arrows show the other three defensive players moving toward their zone positions. The boxed numbers indicate their zone positions. In *Diagram 6-21* the guard has beaten 1 with his dribble and changes direction moving toward the extended *A Area*, 2 moves from the weak side to make the jump-switch. The other players move to their general zone positions. Although 1 and 2 never double team *together*, they may double team with numbers 3, 4, and 5 as is shown in *Diagram 6-16*. Showing a man-to-man defense as the offense moves the ball into the front court, along with the use of the jump-switch involving the chasers, tends to confuse

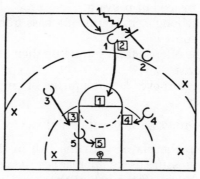

Diagram 6-20

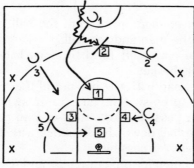

Diagram 6-21

the offense as to what defense is being used and makes this *trap zone* just that much more effective.

The differences between the man-to-man and zone half-court is not easily determined by the offense. In the man-to-man, the jump-switch, fake jump-switch, double team and the number of players involved in the rotation are determined by what the offense does. In the zone, the double team and the jump-switch are determined by the defensive men involved. Both are trying to cause confusion and create a turnover before the offense is able to set up in the offensive lane.

SUMMARY

The half-court man-to-man and zone pressure defense is designed to do the following:

1. Pick up the man with the ball at mid-court.
2. Force the offense to advance the ball to the front court by dribbling instead of passing.
3. Prevent the long or medium long pass from the back court to the front court.
4. Prevent the offense from setting up their offensive patterns in the lane area.
5. Create the turnover, a prerequisite of any good pressure defense today.

These goals may be accomplished by:

1. Picking up the player with the ball in the back court and applying pressure as he approaches the center line.
2. Pick up players off the ball as they cross the center line.
3. Use a preventive or close stance on offensive players "one pass away."
4. If 30 feet or more away from the ball, use an open stance, splitting the man and the ball.
5. Force the player off the ball to go backdoor when moving toward his basket.
6. Keep the man with the ball out of the extended A area.
7. Use the jump-switch, fake jump-switch, or double team whenever possible in the man-to-man pressure.
8. Force the ball down the sidelines with the zone and double team whenever possible.
9. Defensive men forming umbrella and ready for a careless pass out of the double team.

7

Defensive "Stunts" in the Offensive Lane

The jump-switch, fake jump-switch and double team can also be effective in the offensive lane man-to-man defense. If it were not for these "stunts" that are used in the lane man-to-man defense, it would be very much like the man-to-man defense used by many of the top man defensive coaches in the country. The "stunts" are an additional help in making it difficult for opponents to use their regular man-to-man offenses and have the success they desire. Following is an explanation of how they are applied in the lane defense.

BREAKING UP THE TWO MAN PLAYS IN THE OFFENSIVE LANE AREA

Most pattern and even free-lance man-to-man offenses are a series of two-man plays. In the pattern offense there is a set plan on how the other three players get into the offense. In the free-lance offense, there is no set plan for this. Planning, or the lack of it, is the main difference between a pattern and free-lance offense. You can give both of these offenses trouble, if you can break up the two-man plays. Following are a number of ways in which the defense combats these offenses:

1. Using a tough preventive closed stance on players "one pass away." Forcing the outside offensive player out of the lane or forcing the man with the ball to dribble by making his short pass difficult. Using the same stance on the inside offensive players and forcing them out of the no-ball area (*Diagram 7-1*).

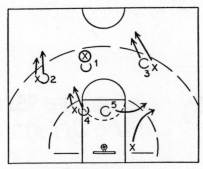

Diagram 7-1

2. Using the jump-switch and double team on the dribbler *(Diagram 7-2)*. Both may be used anywhere in the offensive lane if the opportunity is there.

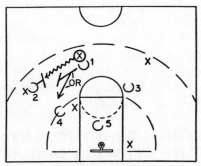

Diagram 7-2

3. Even when they make a successful pass in the lane area and the 1 defensive player is not able to force the passer backdoor, you can stop the two man play if 2 jump-switches before 1's man can get to 2's man to receive a hand-off from him. This may seem to be a dangerous move, leaving the man that already has the ball. However, 1 is moving fast toward 2's man and is between him and the basket a split second after 2 leaves him. Player 2 shouts "go" when he makes this move to alert 1 that he must take the man with the ball. This will definitely play havoc with any pattern or free-lance, two-man play starting with the pass, follow and return pass *(Diagram 7-3)*.

4. Even when 2's man clears out for 1's man to dribble into the no-ball area, sometimes our 2 player will follow his man to the foul lane then turn back to make the jump-switch. This

Diagram 7-3

"stunt" will only be used by 2 when he knows that there is a defensive man on the "help side" near the basket to pick up his man as he moves toward the basket. Player 1 will either move on taking 2's man or double team (*Diagram 7-4*).

Diagram 7-4

DEFENSING THE HIGH POST

When the dribbler tries to use the high post man for a screen, 2 will make a short jump-switch to stop 1's man. If 2's man rolls to the basket, there is no need to worry about a mismatch (which usually occurs). The defense gets help from the "third man on defense." *As soon as the defensive players off the ball see this two-man play developing, the closest player to the basket becomes the third man.* Player 1 moves in between the ball and the player who is "rolling" to the basket. In *Diagram 7-5*, 3 is the third man who helps to defend this two-man play. Player 4 will protect the weakside basket area. On all two-man

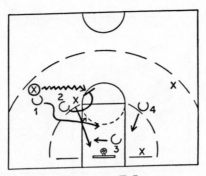

Diagram 7-5

plays in the high post area, the third man is used to protect the basket. It is important that whoever is going to be the third man move into position to help as soon as he sees the switch taking place.

On passes from the *A* to *B* areas into the high post area, 2 (guarding the post) will do one of two things. When the offensive player cuts off the postman to receive the return pass, he will "help and recover" or switch. If the cutter receives the ball, he should switch, but if the postman fakes the pass, he should "help and recover." If the cutter receives the ball and 2 switches, 1 moves between the ball and 2's man as he rolls toward the basket. Player 3 (third man on defense) will help take him. Player 4 will take 3's man (*Diagram 7-6*). Player 3 must get set to help when he sees the two-man plan developing. These "stunts" enable the defense to stay ahead of the offense when executed properly. The men off the ball must be ready when

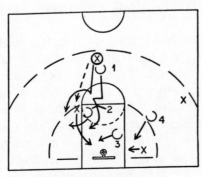

Diagram 7-6

they see the offensive maneuvers developing such as in *Diagram 7-5* and *Diagram 7-6*. If they are alert they will succeed in jamming up the lane area or any path to the basket that would result in a good percentage shot.

The jump-switch or fake jump-switch is used whenever possible. The players even jump-switch when the dribbler is moving from *C* area toward *B* area. This jump-switch, when used sparingly, is very effective. It not only upsets the continuity of the offense, but often results in a "recovery" because the dribbler is usually surprised by this move and often travels, throws a bad pass or charges into the defensive player that made the jump-switch (*Diagram 7-7*). *This also can be a very effective double team.*

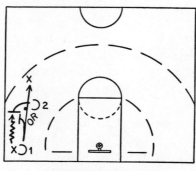

Diagram 7-7

DEFENSING THE "SHUFFLE"

The shuffle offense and similar offenses can give any man-to-man defense problems. Since they are chiefly passing offenses and most of the screens and cutters off the screens come from the weak side, shuffles are difficult to defense. It is not easy to break up the continuity of a good shuffle offense. The best method to defense the initial weak-side cut with the screen is for 4 to back off the screener and check 1's man as he is moving toward the basket until 1 slides through on the ballside of the screen, and picks him up. Player 4 then recovers and takes his own man (help and recovery move). There is no switch here. The defense does switch on all other screens that develop

Diagram 7-8

after this initial screen. The defensive player guarding the man setting up the screen calls the "switch" (*Diagram 7-8*).

We also tried to keep the "shuffle" from getting started by having the players call out "Shuffle" as soon as they saw it developing. Player 2 would now play his man strong to the offensive player's left to prevent the pass to 5's man. Player 5 would force his man as far out as possible to receive the pass. Player 2 and 5 doing this would often break up the rhythm of the "shuffle."

If we were unable to stop the effectiveness of the "shuffle" by using the above methods, or if they were using three or four cycles of it before attempting to score, we would slide into *zone*. *Diagram 7-9* shows how to move into the zone. The best time to change to zone is when the weak-side offensive man uses an initial screen on the high post to start the second cycle of the "shuffle." If *Diagram 7-8* represented the second cycle, the defensive players would be in the position in the zone as shown

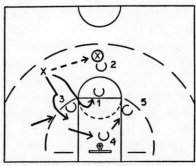

Diagram 7-9

in *Diagram 7-9.* When we had decided to go zone, we would automatically change as they started the second cycle. A change of defense in the middle of a continuity offense can be effective. In the zone, 3, 4 and 5 are able to interchange wingman and baseman positions. Players 1 and 2 were always the "chasers." If the strategy of the opponent is to play a controlled or delayed type of offense, this change can be effective. In this type of offense, you can always go back to man-to-man when opponents change to a zone offense.

DEFENSING THE "STACK" OFFENSE

When the opponents use a "stack" offense as in *Diagram 7-10,* 3 plays directly in front of his man in a half open stance, so he can see both the ball and his man. Player 4 plays on the inside of 4's man and several feet in front of his man. This offense is usually started by 3's or 4's man breaking toward the sideline for the pass from 1's man. No matter who makes this move to receive the pass, 3 takes him and 4 takes the other man. Player 3 tries to prevent the pass, if he can, or at least force the pass receiver as far outside as possible. This defensive strategy has helped prevent good offensive movement in the "stack" offense. Player 3, knowing he is going to guard the man who breaks toward the sideline, is able to gain a step or two and is often able to prevent a successful pass into the desired area. Players 1 and 2 also may use the jump-switch, fake jump-switch, and double team on the two offensive guards when possible.

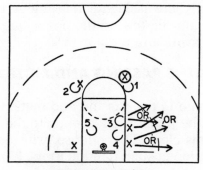

Diagram 7-10

DEFENSING THE "I" OFFENSES

When the offense sets up in the "I" formation or something similar to it, in order to clear out one side for a good dribbling guard, we have three players guard four and 2 will jump-switch or at least fake it. Player 1 will double team about half the time on the jump-switch. If this is not successful in giving this "clear out" offense a difficult time, we will go into our zone when the offensive set indicates this type of offense (*Diagram 7-11*).

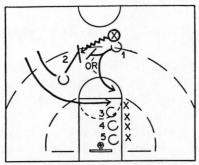

Diagram 7-11

STRAIGHT MAN-TO-MAN DEFENSE
IN THE OFFENSIVE LANE

The defense sometimes plays a *straight man-to-man* in the lane area. *The 2 defensive player will make* the decision. Whenever the *movement is lateral* in the lane area by: (1) the dribbler; (2) the passer moving toward the ball, 1 stays with his man and 2 stays with his. This straight man-to-man is only applicable when there is lateral movement in the lane area. Once the ball is moving toward the no-ball area or inside it, the regular rules of switching are applied.

DEFENSING THE PASSING AND MOTION OFFENSE

Now we come to the passing and motion offense used by everybody from the junior high level up to the pros. Why is this so? The answer is clear. This offense, with its various screens and constant motion in such tight quarters, leads to many illegal screens, which are seldom called and which make it close to impossible to stop the 12- to 18-foot jumper or the eventual roll for the easy lay-up. The constant motion and screening within the no-ball area tends to take away the effectiveness of the weak-side help of any man-to-man defense. Even when the defense does a good job of fighting over screens or switches well, eventually the offense will get the short jumper, which almost all players shoot today with a high percentage of accuracy. This is one of the reasons you see so many 2-3 zones used today by top college and high school teams. This zone is able to push the jump shot out a little further on the court and gives the defense better rebounding position. However, if the opponents have good outside shooters and use an offense that penetrates the gaps in the 2-3, the zone also will fail to do the job. Recently many coaches are finding that a multiple type defense is more effective than any of the conventional zones.

The Amoeba multiple defense can slow this offense effectively when executed properly. Because of the way most of these motion offenses set up, it is an *ideal offense* to change defenses on. The combination of defenses that work best against this offense is as follows:

Whenever possible it is best to start out with the half court man-to-man press that was illustrated in the previous chapter. This first line of defense will make the offense work hard to get to their 1-2-2 set in the no-ball area. The defense remains in the man-to-man until the set offense starts its movement as shown in *Diagram 7-12*.

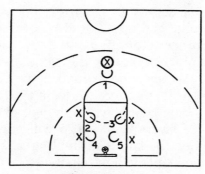

Diagram 7-12

Diagram 7-13

What lane defense to be used is not determined until the players see what the point guard does after his first pass. If he passes and follows as in *Diagram 7-13,* the *defense remains in man-to-man.* Usually when the guard passes and follows he wants to have the forward return the ball to him and this move keys the series of screens that will follow in the offense. Defensive players 1 and 4 will do one of three things on this move: (1) 4 may jump-switch as 2 does in *Diagram 7-3.* If jump is successful, the point guard, the play maker, is unable to get the return hand off from the forward and this will upset the flow of the offense. (2) 1 may double team the ball with 4 as in *Diagram 7-13.* (3) 4 may let 1 slide through and stay with this man. On this pass and follow, the jump-switch or double team will be used about 50 percent of the time. The defense will stay man-to-man until there is a dead ball or a transition takes place.

If the point guard passes and goes away, *the defense will change to zone* as shown in *Diagram 7-14.* These keys are subject to being changed any time it is so desired. If the point guard does any other thing after the pass, such as cut to the basket or just stays in relatively the same area he passes, the defense may play either zone or man depending on the game situation. Player 1 will either double team the ball with 4 or split the passing lane of the guards when changing to zone, as shown in *Diagram 7-14.* Players 2, 3, and 5 will move to off the ball zone positions when the ball is in the *B* area. When a dead ball occurs and the opponents still have possession of the ball as on a jump ball situation or an out-of-bounds, the defense may

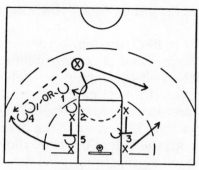

Diagram 7-14

change again depending on what the *keys* are. There are many keys that you can use to determine the defense you wish to use after the initial pass starts the opponent's offense. A very easy key is if the initial pass is made to the right of the defense you go to zone, if to the left, you stay in man-to-man.

This constant changing of defenses can keep the offense from getting into the desired rhythm that is necessary in a well executed motion offense. It also can frustrate the most skilled point guard.

DEFENSING THE FOUR-CORNER OFFENSE

A coach is forced to make one of his most difficult decisions when his team is losing and the opposition goes into the four-corner offense. How should he defense it? To be honest, there is no sure-fire defense to use if the opponents execute the offense well.

Fortunately, the Amoeba defense principles and stunts fit in with what may be the best way to attack this delayed offense. You must first make it as difficult as possible for the two guards to penetrate into the center of the front court by either the dribble or pass. You must then force them into as many double teams as possible along the sidelines and corners with the proper sized "umbrella" flooding the strong side and splitting the passing lanes in an attempt to create a *turnover*. If they are able to penetrate into the center of the front court, avoid the double teams, and keep their "cool," the easy lay-up eventually is inevitable.

The best way to force the four-corner offense to dribble or pass down the sidelines and get opportunities to double-team is to use the Amoeba half-court pressure defense illustrated in detail in Chapter Six. In most cases, when the opponents use this offense they are slow in getting the ball into the front court. This means that at least 75 percent of the time your 1 guard can meet the player with the ball at the centerline. With everybody playing their man tough, this *first* line of defense makes it more difficult for the offense to set-up in their four corner positions. How long the defense remains in man-to-man depends on how soon the defense has its first successful double team. After the first double team the defense will now use the *half-court zone* principles, until there is a dead ball, a recovery, or the offense starts being successful in retaining possession of the ball by using long passes in their four corner set up.

Diagram 7-15 shows an early successful double team. The zone trap is now used until a dead ball, a recovery, or delayed tactics are being successful. If the delay is being successful the defense must go back to man defense and force the ball down the sidelines to get another double team and then zone principles again.

Diagram 7-16 shows that the offense, having been successfully delayed with their four-corner set, is finally forced, by the 2 defensive player, to dribble down the sideline with the help of over-play from his teammates with the man-to-man defense.

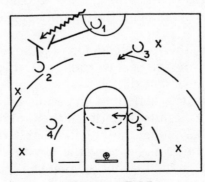

Diagram 7-15

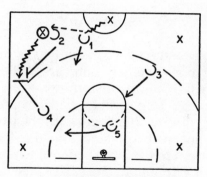

Diagram 7-16

Player 4 makes a jump-switch which always becomes a double team in this defense. Players 1, 3 and 5 umbrella to the strong side, cutting off the passing lanes in an attempt to create a turnover. The defense now uses zone principles until a dead ball, recovery or delayed tactics are being successful again. If the opponents retain possession of the ball when it goes out-of-bounds on the side in the front court, the defense then is the pressure type man-to-man with the 1 defensive player *playing on the ball, double-teaming the point guard,* or playing *centerfield (See Diagram 8-1).*

Again, to repeat, the defense must keep the ball from successfully penetrating into the center of the front court and at the same time shut off the long cross court passes. When the defense does this, it can eventually get the desired double team and the possible recovery.

Most of the time this offense will only shoot the high percentage lay-up, therefore, by protecting the basket at all times whether in zone or man defense, a good defense will eventually force them into a turnover or a shot they do not wish to take.

If time is running short and you are still behind and it is imperative that you gain control of the ball, the players must then foul. Under these circumstances your players must know how to foul by going for the ball and not the offensive player. You should have a drill showing how this can best be done so that you avoid a two-shot "intentional foul" call. (NOTE: Rule change for 1983–84 season makes this strategy obsolete in the last two minutes of the game.)

SUMMARY

The defensive "stunts" add additional strength to our man-to-man defense in the offensive lane area. These "stunts" when used properly, will not only push the pattern offense out of the lane, but may break it up completely. They are especially effective against the patterns that begin with the two-man play, making them also successful against the free-lance offense. The free-lance offenses are usually a series of two-man plays with an excess amount of dribbling. These "stunts" give the dribbling offense all kinds of trouble. They are even troublesome to the pattern offenses that do not begin with the two-man play.

This additional strength to the defense may be accomplished by:

1. Using the jump-switch before the offensive player with the ball can start the two-man play.
2. Using the double team in the proper areas.
3. Using the "third man on defense" on all switches in the high post or near the high post area.
4. Using the jump-switch, even when the offense "clears out" in the lane area.
5. Changing defenses after the offense is in motion.
6. Forcing the defense off the ball to go backdoor on move toward the basket.
7. Use a multiple half-court pressure defense against a slow-up offense such as the "four-corners."

8

Full and Three-Quarter Court Man-to-Man and Zone Pressure Defense

WHY THE AMOEBA PRESS IS SUCCESSFUL

Most pressing defenses may be effective when used for short periods of time during a game. How effective they are is usually determined by how well the opposing coach has prepared his players in attacking the press that is being used. For example, good preparation for attacking a 1-2-1-1 full court zone press and proper execution by the players will render it helpless; the ball will move swiftly into the front court without the desired turnover the defense is trying to create. Most teams today are thoroughly drilled on how to break each and every type of press, because coaches know that if they are able to get a lead in any game, sooner or later their opponent is going to press them. They also know that if their players do not get upset by the pressure applied and execute the planned attack properly, the press should not be too effective.

If a team is beaten by a pressing defense it is usually for one of two reasons: (1) the coach did not have them prepared for it, and/or (2) the players were upset by the pressure and did not execute the planned attack properly. The point I am trying to get to is, if the coach *knows the type of press he will be playing against* and his players follow his planned attack well, the chance of its causing a problem is small.

The advantage the Ameoba full and three-quarter press has over the other presses is that the coach has a more difficult time preparing his players to play against it. The constant changing of the defensive pressure being used makes it difficult to plan any certain set offense against it. The Amoeba press uses a combination of zone and man-to-man principles in such a way that the opposition is unable to use one set offensive pattern to attack it. Following is an explanation of how it operates:

The first line of defense in the press begins whenever the ball is taken out-of-bounds in the backcourt. Most of the time it will begin with over-guarding man-to-man pressure. The only difference in the full court pressure from the three-quarter is that the full court *will make every attempt to keep the pass from being inbounded successfully*. The three-quarter will *fake that attempt* then let the pass be inbounded. After the ball is inbounded successfully, the second line of defense will be determined by whatever *keys* are being used. It may be the man-to-man press with the jump-switch, fake jump-switch and double team or the zone press (1-2-1-1, 2-1-2, or 2-2-1). When the multiple defense is executed properly, it is difficult for the players and especially their point guard to determine what defense is being used.

DEFENSING THE INBOUND PASS

Regardless of what the defense will be, zone or man, the first line of defense will show a man-to-man set when the ball is out-of-bounds. The 1 defensive player will be in one of three positions: (1) on the ball, (2) *double-teaming the point guard,* (3) *playing centerfield (Diagram 8-1).* What position he plays the most is determined by the game situation. The alignment's main strategy is to make the inbound pass as difficult as possible. Defensive players 4 and 5 will be splitting their man in such a way as to prevent the long pass and attempt to keep him from receiving the inbound pass by moving to the backcourt. The same defensive alignment is used when the ball is taken out-of-bounds on the side as shown in *Diagram 8-1. It shows 1 in all three defense positions. The position that 1 plays could be the key to determine what type of press will be used or what defense will be played when the offense gets to the offensive lane.* As was mentioned, there are many keys that can be used in determining the defense to be used, and this is one of them.

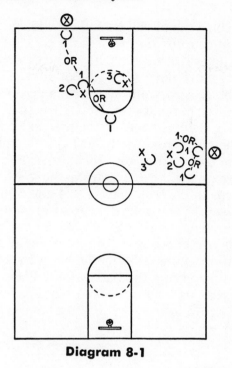

Diagram 8-1

FULL AND THREE-QUARTERS MAN-TO-MAN PRESS

When playing the man-to-man press, the decision on whether to go full or three-quarter court depends on the offense the opponents use or the speed and cleverness of their offensive guards. In general, the defensive tactics are determined by the type of offensive press attack used by the opponents. The various press attacks that may be used are classified into five distinct categories: (1) 1-4 press attack; (2) 2-3; (3) 3-2; (4) 4-1; and (5) 5-0 (number of offensive players set up in backcourt = number set up in front-court). The defense can be explained best by showing the strategy in each of these offensive press attacks.

Defensing the 1-4 Offensive Press Attack

When the pass is successfully inbounded, the second line of defense is set. When the defense shows man-to-man, most offenses will first use the *clear out offense* or the *1-4 press attack.* The point guard will go one on one and attempt to dribble to the front court on his own. The *A* area is extended into the back court when pressing full court. The defense does not want the offense to move down this 12-foot alley. The defense must force the dribbler across this alley or if a player receives the ball in this alley force him out of it. Notice the position of 3, 4 and 5 (*Diagram* 8-2). Each is splitting the ball and his man in accordance with their distance from the ball; 2's and 3's men have cleared out and moved to the front court. Player 2 follows his man to approximately 15 feet from the center line and then stops and turns to the ball. Players 3, 4 and 5 must defense four offensive players. They split their men in such a way that this can be accomplished while the *ball is in the deep back court.* Since the defense player is in front of his man, he is able to stay with his man much better when his man tries to move into the back court to help bring the ball over the center line. He is also in a better position to intercept a careless lob or long pass. Players 3, 4 and 5 are always looking for the *lob* or long pass.

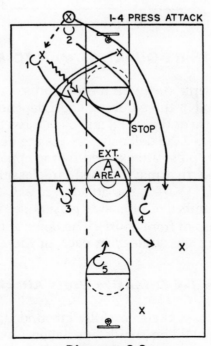

Diagram 8-2

Players 3 and 4 would be looking for either the lob or long pass to 2's man. Player 5 would be looking for the same on the pass to 3's or 4's man. Player 2's man cleared out so the offensive guard can dribble the ball to the front court in a one-to-one situation. The 1 defensive player plays the dribbler toward the center of the court and 2, who stopped following his man approximately six feet beyond the top of the key, reverses his movement and makes the jump-switch. Player 1 has a choice of moving to the front court or double-teaming the dribbler. In *Diagram 8-2*, 1 moves to the front court. There are three defensive men involved in this jump-switch as 4 takes 2's man and 1 takes 4's man.

Diagram 8-2 also shows 1 double-teaming on this jump-switch with 2. As soon as 3, 4 and 5 see the double team, they move up a few feet and umbrella the floor. When the offense is using the 1-4 press attack against the man-to-man, the players may double-team anywhere in the back court, even the center of the floor. This is especially true deep in the back court. If an offensive player seeing the situation moves to the back court to help, the closest defensive player goes with him. The players are instructed on a double team not to reach in, but to flail their arms wildly and force the player with the ball to pass weakly or erratically. If the dribbler starts playing with his dribble, 2 may *fake* the jump-switch and keep splitting the ball and his man, retreating slowly as the dribbler cautiously moves toward the front court. If their 1 guard is worrying more about the defense than getting the ball to his teammates, the press is being effective. *Players should be taught that a recovery (or "steal") is the bonus of a good pressing defense, not a necessity.*

Defensing the 2-3 Offensive Press Attack

Diagram 8-3 shows the defensive movement against a 2-3 press attack. Player 1 forces the dribbler toward the 2 defensive player. If 2 jump-switches as indicated in the diagram, 1 moves on to take 2's man. Player 2's man moves toward the front court. Player 1 also continues toward the front court. If the jump-switch was successful in stopping the dribbler, he may try to pass to 2's man, but 3 has moved up and has him covered (this is often a good recovery when he does pass). On the 2-3 attack,

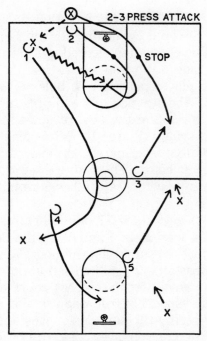

Diagram 8-3

*since 3's man was the last offensive player to cross the center
line to the front court, 3 stops near the center line.* Players 4 and
5 will split their men so they can guard the three players in the
front court. This diagram shows a counter-clockwise rotation of
all five defensive players. This doesn't happen very often, but
when the position of the players is such that 3, 4 and 5 do not
have to move very far to accomplish it, it is very effective. Player
3 takes 2's man, 5 moves up and covers 3's man, and 4 moves
back and takes 5's man, necessitating 1 to cover 4's man. This
represents a complete chain reaction with all five players involved. Since the dribbler is moving to the defense's right, all the
players to the right, which would be considered the strong side,
move toward the ball. The one player on the weak side (4) moves
toward the basket. In this particular situation 2 made the jump-
switch, but he had two other choices. He could have stayed with
his man and made his jump-switch near the center line or just
as he crossed it or he could have faked the jump-switch and
stayed with his man. He may have used four or five fakes as the

dribbler moved toward the offensive lane area. It must be remembered that if 2's man did not move toward center and 3,
there would be only a two-man switch and 1 would have taken
2's man.

When using the *full* court pressure, the defensive player
making an attempt to intercept the inbound pass may be out of
position and unable to force the dribbler toward the center of the
floor. This is what took place in *Diagram 8-4*. When this happens, the defense is ready to set the double team at the center
line. Player 4 now becomes 2 in the movement, as the dribbler
moves across the center line. Player 4 makes the jump-switch
and 1 double-teams with him while 2, 3 and 5 move into the
umbrella. This is an ideal spot for the double team on the dribbler. When 3 sees the double team forming, he shouts "I'll take
5," and 5 moves out in an attempt to intercept the pass if it is
made to 4's man. Player 2 is ready for any careless pass near the
center circle. Player 5 is the only defensive player who cannot
gamble in this defense. He must *never* leave the basket area on a

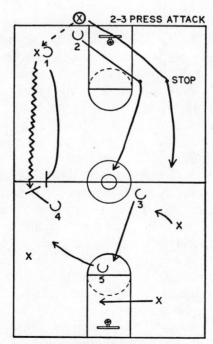

Diagram 8-4

switch, if he isn't certain a teammate is on the way and close enough to protect the basket. In this particular move 3 was able to cover 5's area. In both of these defensive moves in *Diagrams 3 and 4,* if the point guard passes to a teammate successfully, the defense with its jump-switch, fake jump-switch and the double team will continue even when the offense is moving in the offensive lane.

Sometimes an opponent using the 2-3 attack will have 2's man, when 2 makes his jump-switch, loop back to the weak side. Player 2's man moves toward the center line as if he is clearing out for the dribbler, but he *stops* before he gets to center court. When 2 makes his jump-switch, his man makes a quick move to the weak side. It is difficult for 1 to cover 2's man when he loops like this. Players 3 or 4 cannot take him soon enough because they are too far away. Regardless of what 1 does, move to the front court or double team, the dribbler can stop and make a short pass to 3's man. However, this move need not take the pressure off the offense.

There are several ways to counteract this "loop" move: (1) 2 fakes a jump-switch and if his man makes the loop, he stays with him and splits the passing lane as illustrated in *Diagram 8-5.* Even if the pass is successfully made to the player that looped, the ball has not advanced to the front court and the defense is able to start pushing him into another jump-switch or double team; (2) if the dribbler hesitates and keeps his dribble on 2's fake, 1 keeps forcing the dribbler, so he will move toward the sideline. Player 3 is now ready to make the jump-switch. Player 1 will usually double-team here, because this is one of the better places for it *(Diagram 8-5).* Numbers 2, 4, and 5 will "umbrella" as shown in the diagram. (3) If opponents continue to "loop" by having 2's man go deeper into the back court to receive the pass from the dribbler, 2 makes the jump-switch. Player 1 is now ready for this "loop" and "button hooks" back, but does not try to prevent the dribbler from passing back to his man. However, as soon as his man receives the pass from the dribbler, he is on him tight and forcing him to dribble toward the center, so we may be able to jump-switch, fake jump-switch, or double-team *(Diagram 8-6). Any time the opponents are not advancing the ball the press is successful.* The longer the of-

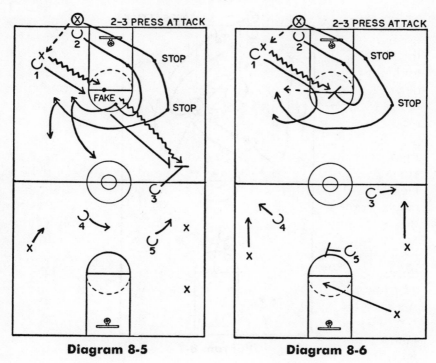

Diagram 8-5   **Diagram 8-6**

fense keeps playing around in the back court with the ball the better. The more passes they use in the deep back court, the higher the risk for turning the ball over. There is also the ten-second rule, which this defense has caused many teams to violate over the years. The flexibility of this press makes it possible to adjust to any offense the opponents may use.

Defensing the 3-2 Offensive Press Attack

In the 3-2 attack against the press the opponents will bring a third man into the back court (*Diagram 8-7*). Player 4 stops near the center line. Player 5, splitting his man, guards the two offensive players when the ball is in the deep back court. Now there are all kinds of possibilities. The player receiving the inbound ball passes immediately to 3's man. Player 3 pushes his man toward the sideline. Player 2 jump-switches and his man moves toward the front court. Number 4 takes 2's man, and 3

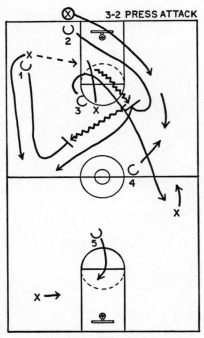

Diagram 8-7

takes 4's man. There are three defensive players involved in this rotation. The dribbler does not stop this time, but changes direction. Player 1, as he is moving toward the front court with his man, seeing the dribbler changing direction and moving toward him, "button hooks" back and makes a jump-switch. There are only two defensive players in this jump-switch. This is usually a very effective jump-switch. The dribbler is usually taken by surprise because he is not expecting 1 to change direction; the jump-switch catches him in full motion so that he will often charge into 1. Player 2 moves on down and takes 1's man. Player 5 moves back to protect the basket and to be closer to his man. It is possible that if the dribbler changed direction again, 3, after taking 4's man, would make the jump-switch near the center line. When there are three or more offensive players in the back court there are more opportunities to use the different defensive moves. If the offensive guard is starting to have success by breaking our press by reversing direction on his dribble, 1 may double-team him more often. We may say, "Double-team every other time or do it the next two times he brings the ball up the floor." When three or more players move to the back court to get the ball through the press, chances are they will try to do it by passing. The more passing there is in the back court, the higher the risk of additional errors when pressured. The opponent must not be successful with the *long* pass. When a long pass is successful, someone is not doing his job. When positioning is correct, there is a good chance to intercept it. This is accomplished by balanced spacing of the players on the floor and their alertness to the possibility of the long pass. *It is a must in the defense for the players to turn toward the ball as they cross the center line going back on defense* in a sliding, gliding movement.

Defensing the 4-1 Offensive Press Attack

When an opponent uses the 4-1 attack, the defense gets ready for a variety of screens by the three players in the back court. The players are instructed not to fight through them but to switch. In *Diagram 8-8,* 4's man is setting the screen on 3; 4

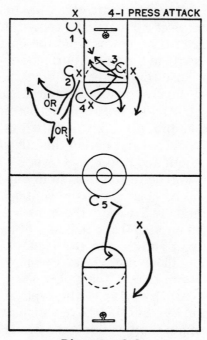

Diagram 8-8

would call the switch. I will not discuss all the different combinations of screens they could use; it is sufficient to say that the players should be told when three or four offensive players set up in the back court to operate against the press, to be alert for the screens and the long pass. Player 5 is not as far out in front of his man as he would be ordinarily. In this offense the opponents often attempt the long pass to get the easy lay-up. When 5 is the only defensive player in the front court, he must always be alert for this. He must also be looking for the long pass to 2's man and 3's man, if they happen to get ahead of their defensive men. The long pass may be thrown by either the out-of-bounds player or the player receiving the short pass in-bounds. When the opponents are unable to use the long pass, this defense is very successful against the 4-1 press attack. There are additional opportunities for the jump-switch, fake jump-switch and double team.

Defending the 5-0 Offensive Press Attack

When the opponents bring the fifth man into the back court, the offensive set up is usually something like you see in *Diagram 8-9.* Player 5 never goes into the back court when the offensive man sets up in the front court and moves into the back court. When they use this method to break the press, 1 moves from the baseline area to the top of the foul circle. He opens up so he can see the ball and 5's man. When 5's man moves into the back court, 1 picks him up to prevent the out-of-bounds player from passing to him. If 1 did not do this they could receive the inbound pass without any pressure. Player 5's man would come down the center to receive the pass from out-of-bounds. Player 2's and 4's man, who cleared out the center by moving toward the sidelines, would break toward the front court. Another familiar formation used in the 5-0 attack is also illustrated in *Diagram 8-9.* When 5's man comes into the back court to set up the offense, 5 will not follow him. Player 1 will guard 5's man (as in *Diagram 8-9*). Number 5 is the safety valve in this offensive formation. They usually will set the type of screens that are shown in *Diagram 8-9,* but they have various other moves out of this set up. The main thing the defense wants to prevent here is

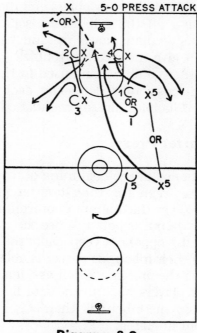

Diagram 8-9

the successful long pass. Player 1, 3 and 5 should be ready to prevent it.

The more offensive players in the back court, the more opportunities the defense has in using the jump-switch, fake jump-switch and double team. The main overall strategy is to keep the offensive guards guessing. This press seldom looks the same two times in a row.

When the offense tries to break the press by bringing their big man deep in the back court to receive the short pass from out-of-bounds, they want him to hold the ball high above his head with two hands. Regardless of the pressure applied, he eventually will find an open player near the center of the court or further and pass to him. This can be a successful maneuver, but can be counteracted by having the defensive player guarding the big man drop off about 20 to 25 feet, leaving him wide open. There are now five men guarding four and it is now more difficult to pass up court. If he is forced to start dribbling toward the front court the defense is ready. There are not too many *big men* who are good back court dribblers and they are also not too accurate in passing off the dribble. As soon as he starts his dribble the defensive man moves up and harasses him. This counteraction can give the offense trouble.

There are other combinations used in these *five* offensive set ups, but a discussion of defensing each one would be a repetition of the principles already mentioned.

The Three-Quarter Press

It was mentioned at the beginning of this chapter that the only difference between the three-quarter press and the full was that defense *fakes* the attempt to prevent the inbound pass. There are times when it is better to use the three-quarter press than the full. If the opponent (especially the point guard) has great speed, or if their inbounds passer is able to make a quick, accurate pass over the first line of defense, it is then necessary to pull the 1 and 2 players back to the foul line or even further. They let the pass come inbounds, then begin to apply the pressure near the foul line area.

The 1 defensive player ordinarily plays the dribbler strong on one side or the other, so he can force him to dribble toward the center or toward the 2 defensive player. However, if his speed is beating the defensive player and he is able to go down the 12-foot alley of *A* area extended, the defensive player must begin to play him head-on. When the 1 offensive guard possesses this kind of speed and skill, the 1 defensive player is instructed to make it as difficult as possible for him to move toward the front court with his dribble. The defense should also double team this type of dribbler as much as possible. This also means that the dribbler is able to go either way on his defensive player. Now both 2 and 3 must be ready to make the jump-switch if the dribbler moves in his direction.

PLAYERS' RESPONSIBILITIES IN THE PRESS

The responsibilities of each player in our pressing defense are the same whether we are in full, three-quarter, or half court press. They are as follows:

No. 1 Defensive Player

1. Prevent pass to 1 offensive guard whenever possible.
2. Push the dribbler toward the center or closest defensive player.
3. Prevent the dribbler from going down the 12-foot alley (*A* area extended).
4. On the jump-switch, find the open man down court as quickly as possible. When not sure where he is, always head for the no-ball area.
5. On the jump-switch, double team in the double team areas. When it is not in accepted areas, do it only when instructed.
6. Be alert for teammates' commands when guarding the dribbler.
7. Follow the rules on reaching for the ball.

No. 2 Defensive Player

1. Initiate jump-switch.
2. Jump-switch only when the dribbler is coming toward you or in that general direction. Exception is if the dribbler turns back on the defensive player and is near the sidelines or center line and you are close.
3. Double team when 1's man has stopped in double team area if close enough to the area to do it immediately.
4. Keep the length of the jump-switch as short as possible in the front court.
5. Do not cross over from the weak side to make the jump-switch in the front court.
6. Use the *fake jump-switch* when the dribbler retains the dribble and moves forward hesitantly.
7. Shout *"GO"* on all jump-switches.
8. Use closed stance in guarding your man if he is closer to the offensive baseline than the ball.
9. In a 1-4 offense against the press, stop and turn to the ball about half way between the top of the foul circle and the center line.

No. 3 Defensive Player

1. Take 2's man if he is moving toward you or close enough to do it conveniently, when 2 is making his jump-switch.
2. Split your man and the ball the appropriate distance in relation to the ball, your man, and the offensive basket.

3. Be ready to become 1, if your man receives the ball, and 2, 4 or 5 if the offense changes directions.
4. In a 2-3 offense against the press, station yourself near the center of the court. Players 4 and 5 will guard three men while the ball is deep in the back court.
5. On the double team, umbrella the ball in accordance with your location on the floor.
6. Always be alert for the long pass or lob.

No. 4 Defensive Player

1. Take 2's and 3's man if he is moving toward you or close enough to do it conveniently.
2. Split your man and the ball the appropriate distance in relation to the ball, your man, and the offensive basket.
3. Be ready to become 1 if your man receives the ball, and 2, 3 or 5 if the offense changes directions.
4. In the 3-2 offense against the press, station yourself near the center of the court. Player 5 will guard two men while the ball is deep in the back court.
5. In the double team, umbrella the ball in accordance with your location on the floor.
6. Always be alert for the long pass and the lob.

No. 5 Defensive Player

1. Protect the basket *at all times* when a teammate is unable to replace you.
2. Split your man and the ball the appropriate distance in relation to the ball, your man, and the offensive basket.
3. Take 2's, 3's or 4's open man only when you know a teammate can become 5 and protect the basket.
4. Only gamble to steal a pass when you know a teammate is in position to become 5.
5. Never follow your man from the front court to the back court when the offense is using a 4-1 set up against the press.
6. On the double team, umbrella the ball in accordance with your location on the floor.
7. Always be alert for the long pass and lob.

FULL AND THREE-QUARTER ZONE PRESS

The main difference in the zone press from the man-to-man press in the Amoeba defense is the use of the double team.

When the key, whatever it may be, denotes a zone press, the defense will be using the principles employed by the three most popular zone presses tdoay, the 1-2-1-1 and the 2-1-2 or 2-2-1.

Full Court Zone Press

In the full court zone press, the players line up man-to-man and make every attempt to keep the pass from being success-fully inbounded, except when the player moves to the corner. As soon as the defense player sees that his man is heading to the corner in his attempt to get open, he drops off to let his man receive the pass. When he receives the pass, the 1-2-1-1 zone goes into action. Player 1 moves with the pass and double teams with 2. For that matter, the *key* for using the 1-2-1-1 may be when 1 double teams with 2 on the inbound pass. The defense will now double team when possible, the whole length of the court down either side line until they go into their offensive lane defense, be it man or zone. *If the key* was the double team in the corner by 1, this would signal the other four defensive players to use the zone principles with the double team until the offense set up in the offensive lane.

See *Diagrams 8-10* and *8-11*. In *Diagram 8-10* it shows 2 stopping so his man will be open, then forming a double team with 1. *Diagram 10* also shows 3 and 4 in the umbrella just close enough to the two offensive players that should receive the pass out of the double team to have the opportunity to steal an erratic or careless pass. Player 5 protects the front court and is ready for any long pass. *Diagram 11* shows the next possible double team if the ball is passed down the sidelines. *The out-of-bounds defen-sive alignment is the same as the on the ball, full court man-to-man press (Diagram 8-1).* This flexibility in the defense keeps the offense guessing. There will be no man-to-man cover-age after the inbound pass, only the double team and zone prin-ciples off the ball the whole way down the court to the offensive lane. This is the *full court zone press.*

Three-Quarter Zone Press

In the three-quarter zone press the defense still plays man-to-man on the inbound pass, but there is no man on the out-of-bounds player *(Diagram 8-12). This formation is the*

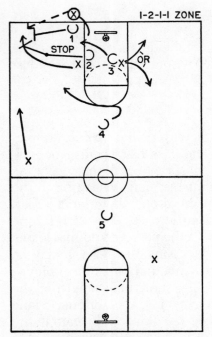

Diagram 8-10

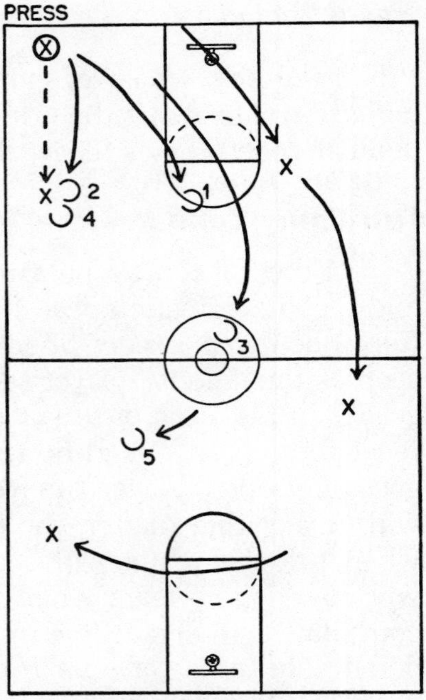

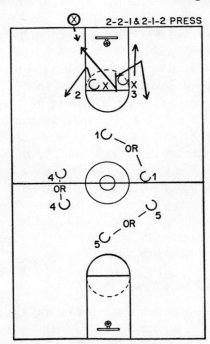

Diagram 8-11

Diagram 8-12

same as the centerfield position in our man-to-man defense (*Diagram 8-1*). In the three-quarter zone, 2 and 3 only go a few steps with their man, then immediately drop back to beyond the foul line extended. Where 1, 4 and 5 move after the pass is inbounded depends on which zone will be played, the 2-1-2 or 2-2-1 (*Diagram 8-12*). These two zones will be semi-aggressive until the double team is formed. Players 2 and 3 will fake at the guard with the ball and then drop back, much the same as the fake jump-switch in the man-to-man defense. Players 1, 4 and 5 will also move back toward offensive lane keeping the relative positions of the 2-1-2 or 2-2-1 zone.

These two defenses attempt to keep the ball out of the center and push the ball down the sidelines by a pass or dribble. If they are successful in doing this, they will attempt to double team, if the opportunity is there. *Another object of this three quarter zone press is to slow up the transition play of the opponents.* It is very successful in doing this. The press may double team along the sidelines the whole way down court to the corner of the offense lane. *Diagram 8-13* shows three of the possible

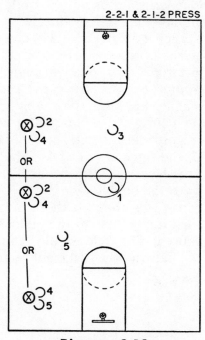

2-2-1 & 2-1-2 PRESS

Diagram 8-13

double teams. *Only the umbrella formed (3, 1 and 5) is shown off the double team in the back court of the diagram.* On all the double teams the three defensive players forming the umbrella jam the strong or ball side as much as possible.

SUMMARY

The full court man-to-man pressure defense is designed to apply pressure on the ball and the other four offensive players before the ball is put into play from out-of-bounds deep in the back court. The three-quarter man press is designed to do the same thing as soon as the inbound pass has been received by an offensive player.

How the pressure is applied depends upon the type of offense used by the opponents. The flexibility in the press is accomplished by varying the use of the jump-switch, fake jump-switch and the double team. How the players apply each of these defensive moves is determined by the offense used. Each variation in the offense may give the defense a "new look." For example, if the opponents are using a 1-4 offense, the defense will attempt to double team the 1 offensive guard more often *anywhere* in the back court. For each change the offense makes, the man-to-man pressure defense changes with it.

The full court *zone* press shows man-to-man coverage when the ball is out-of-bounds. Once the pass is inbounded, zone pressing principles featuring the double team are used the whole length of the court. The three-quarter zone press shows man-to-man coverage when the ball is out-of-bounds. After the pass is inbounded, the three-quarter fakes the use of pressure, attempts to push the ball down the sidelines, and if successful applies pressure with the double team.

After the offense gets through these presses, the type of defense used against the offense in the offensive lane depends on the *key* being used. The defense also could change every time there is a dead ball and the opponent retains possession of the ball.

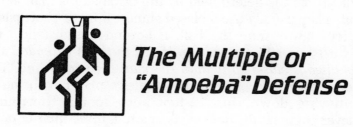

9

The Multiple or "Amoeba" Defense

WHY "AMOEBA"?

The dictionary describes an amoeba as a one-celled animal that moves by forming temporary projections that are constantly changing. After a game with George Washington during the 1971–72 basketball season, the George Washington basketball coach, Carl Sloan, said, "Pitt's defense is just like an amoeba. It is constantly changing." The analogy between the one-celled animal and the combination defense is so accurate that it would be difficult to find a better name than "Amoeba."

This defense *is* constantly changing. At least it seems to be, even when the ball is live and the offense is in the process of moving toward their basket. This is due to the jump-switch and the many defensive options that the players have as a result of this move. Of course, there are "keys" that also dictate what the defense will be playing by the time the offense reaches the offensive lane. By using "keys" and the options determined by the players, *the defense is literally changing constantly.*

MAN-TO-MAN PRINCIPLES

With a few exceptions, this defense is man-to-man when the ball is in the back court, whether it is in bounds or out-of-bounds. Every player is assigned to guard a particular offensive player. However, the only player who *always* plays between his

man and the opponent's basket is the 1 defensive player. He is
guarding the player with the ball. The defensive players off the
ball split their men. How far any defensive player moves out in
front of his man is determined by the distance his man is from
the ball. They usually use a closed stance, if it is a short pass (9
to 15 feet) away from the ball; if beyond this distance, they
usually assume an open stance. *If not in the A extended area,
each is always closer to it than the man he is guarding.* Their
secondary duty is to prevent the offensive player with the ball
from moving down this 12-foot alley to the front court.
Whenever possible, the defense is in a full, three-quarter or half
court press. In general, the only time the defense goes directly
back into the offensive lane defense is when they are unable to
set up any of the three pressing defenses. The defense is able to
use one of the three presses a good deal of the time, because of
one rule we insisted the players abide by at all times: get to your
man *immediately* after your opponents gain possession of the
ball. Even better, get to your man when you can see this transition is going to take place. When the ball finally crosses the
center line, the players, in most defensive alignments, are still
playing man-to-man defense. Once they get close or in the offensive lane area, the keys determine if they are playing zone or
man-to-man.

When the ball is out-of-bounds in the front court on either
side, the defense is *always* man-to-man. When the ball is out at
the end line under the opponent's basket, the defense is *always*
zone. However, the defense may change as soon as the ball is
received in bounds from zone to man-to-man or vice-versa depending on the *keys*.

The Amoeba zone defense makes it possible for the players
to delay looking like a zone defense until the opponents have the
ball in the offensive lane area or very close to it. When playing
the half court pressure defense, the defense is usually man-to-
man when the opponents bring the ball over the center line. As
the ball comes into the front court, the players use the jump-
switch or double team if they can, no matter which defense is
eventually played. These two maneuvers along with the *fake*
jump-switch help hide the defense that they will finally be using.

CHANGING DEFENSES

Diagram 9-1 shows how the players slide into the zone defense after the jump-switch. They attempt to make it look like man-to-man until the ball is in the offensive lane or as long as possible. The arrows show the path of the defensive players when the offense moves on to the lane area after the jump-switch. Player 1 tries to force the dribbler toward 2, who is a chaser in the zone defense. Players 3 and 4 are wingmen and 5 is the baseman. *Diagram 9-1* also shows the defensive players in their zone positions.

Diagram 9-2 shows the dribbler moving toward 3, a wingman. Player 3 jump-switches and 1 double teams with him. In the half court press, when the *key* indicates they will eventually be in a zone, the chasers will jump-switch whenever possi-

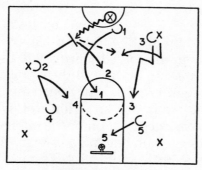

Diagram 9-1

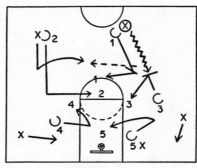

Diagram 9-2

ble but will *never* double team together. When a wingman
makes the jump-switch with a chaser they will *always* double
team. When the offense breaks the double team successfully,
Diagram 9-2 also shows the way the players move to their zone
positions.

When going from man-to-man to a zone, often either 3 or 4
(ordinarily wingmen) may be with his man near the basket in
5's area, while 5 is away from the basket guarding his man. In
this case, 3 or 4 shouts "I'll take *five*." Player 5 would then only
have to move into the open wing spot of 3 or 4. When teaching
the zone, 3, 4 and 5 must learn both the wingman and baseman
positions.

Diagram 9-3 illustrates how 2 fakes the jump-switch and
then moves back to the 2 position in the zone. Arrows show 3
and 5 moving to their proper positions. The dribbler keeps
dribbling and enters the lane area. When he continues to move
through the lane area, 4 (wingman) moves out and there is the
regular double team of the offensive player in the *B* area that
often takes place in the zone. *Diagram 9-3* also shows the three
other defensive players moving to their proper zone positions.

This defense tries to keep the opponents from passing from
the back court to the front court. However, when they do make
this pass, if the pass does not enter the offensive lane or no-ball
area, the players can still play man-to-man until they finally do
enter these areas. In *Diagram 9-4* 2's man received the pass
from the back court. Player 2's man passes the ball to 4's man,
and the defensive players move to their zone positions. Player 2
does not double team this time but fronts player at high post.

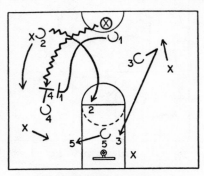

Diagram 9-3

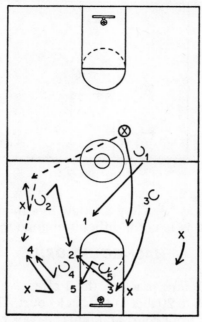

Diagram 9-4

Player 1 splits passing lane to other guard. The position of the players in the zone is also shown in *Diagram 9-4*. The defense must prevent the successful pass from the back court into the lane or no-ball area. The players are ready for this pass at all times and should prevent it as much as possible.

When the ball is out-of-bounds on the side in both the back and front court, the defense is man-to-man and makes it as difficult as possible for the offense to throw the inbound pass. Defensive player 1 plays one of the three positions mentioned before—*on the ball, double team* or *centerfield*. The longer the defense can keep from going into the zone, the more confusing our defense can be. Sometimes the defense may change from zone to man-to-man when the opponents are working the ball in the offensive lane area. This change may be *keyed* when a pass goes from one certain area to another certain area. Example— strong side *B* to strong side *C*. *Diagram 9-5* shows the position of the players in the zone when the ball is in the *B* area. X^1 *passes to X^5 in the C area*. Player 5 takes X^5, 1 has X^1, 4 fronts X^4, 1

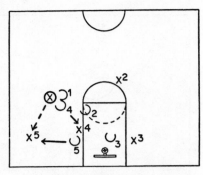

Diagram 9-5

takes X¹ and 3 has X³. They are now in a man-to-man defense. With practice, this is not a difficult change to make.

HALF-COURT DRILL

In the half-court practice, the 1 offensive guard starts with the ball about 15 to 20 feet in the back court. The offense sets up any place in the front court and into the back court. All offensive players should be closer to the basket than the offensive player with the ball.

DRILLS ON MULTIPLE DEFENSE

Diagram 9-6 illustrates how the offense may set up. Player 3's man is in three different positions, 2, 4, and 5's in two positions. The offensive players without the ball can set up any place they desire. This drill gives the defense practice first in keeping the opponents out of the offensive lane and second in changing the defenses smoothly when the key tells them to do so. A coach standing in the back court gives the signal of the defense that will be used when the offense enters the lane area each time before the offense begins its attack. The offense will now try to penetrate the defense and score. The defense uses all the defensive stunts they know in trying to keep the offense from getting into the offensive lane. When the offense gets into the lane area, the defense then goes into the defense the coach signaled. The 1 offensive guard will try to throw long passes when he can. This type of pass must be held to a minimum. When the players

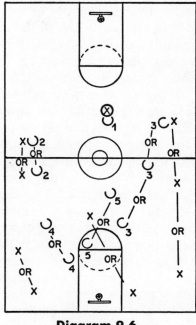

Diagram 9-6

position themselves properly and are alert, the long pass is seldom successful. The defense gets practice against every possible method an opponent might try in order to get their offense started. This changing from one defense to another is not as difficult as it may seem. The jump-switch, fake jump-switch and the double team used by both zone and man-to-man defenses makes them so similar that the opponents may not know the defense has changed until they have made three or four passes.

TRANSITION DRILL

In today's game, this transition takes place from 60 to 90 times or more each game. One of the most difficult jobs for a coach is to have his players execute the transition properly. This is especially true in the transition from offense to defense. For *five* players to go from playing offensive basketball to defensive basketball *correctly* is not easy. Some coaches may say it is impossible. It is certainly true, because of the psychological aspect of changing from offense (fun) to defense (work), most players will not make the transition with the zeal that a coach would desire. Very few players naturally go all out when this transition takes place. It would be safe to say that at least one-third of all field goals in most games are scored as a result of one player or more not being defensively alert immediately after this transition takes place. How then can you get the best effort out of five players in this important phase of defense?

I will answer that question by first asking another question. How do you know when you are getting the best effort out of your players in this transition from offense to defense? I believe one of the better ways to *judge* whether you are getting the effort desired is by instructing the players to get to their men as soon as they know the transition is going to take place. Regardless of whether the transition takes place on a made or missed field goal, or any other way, the players must attempt to be on their men by the time each crosses the center line. This is not possible all the time, but it can definitely be determined when they are not making a sincere effort to do so.

FULL-COURT DRILL

Whenever possible, the defense is pressuring the player with the ball. Even when playing the half-court pressure, 1 is instructed to be on his man as soon as he receives the ball in the back court. He will then slide along with him to the center line and then apply pressure as he crosses it.

Over the years, I found players forming a positive attitude toward playing the defense. *They seem to enjoy the teamwork it takes to make this multiple defense work.* The defense is designed so that when a player makes a defensive mistake (gambles and fails) *he most always gets help from a teammate to cover the mistake. Although it is definitely a team defense, the players feel free to operate defensively as an individual. Each situation may provide the option of two or three different defensive moves.*

In these transition drills, the defense gets practice on the full, three-quarter and half-court press or when desired also the offensive lane defense. The defense also will get practice in going from zone to man-to-man and vice versa. The drills use all the different transition possibilities that come up in a regular game (Diagram 9-7). The coach takes an outside shot. If the ball goes in, the offense takes the ball out. The defense plays the full or three-quarter press. If the ball misses and the opponents get the rebound, all the defensive players get to their men as quickly as possible and try to at least be able to press at half-court. The defense used is determine by the keys and the choices the defensive players make.

A player shoots a foul. Whether it is missed or made, each defensive player goes immediately to the man he is guarding.

The ball is taken out-of-bounds in the back court. The defense, in the full court press, tries to make the inbound difficult, so each player tries to deny his man receiving the pass. Player 2 may be on the ball, centerfield, or double team on the number 1

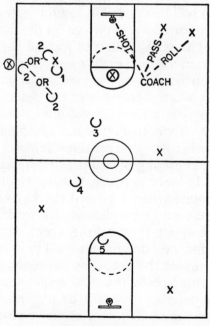

Diagram 9-7

offensive guard. This usually brings more offensive players into the back court. The defense can be more effective with the forwards and center in the back court with the ball.

A loose ball and a turnover are two other transitions that are involved in this drill. The coach has the ball around the top of the foul circle. He fakes a shot and either rolls the ball on the floor or passes the ball to a player on the team working against the defense. This gives the players the actual surprise element of a game situation when a pass is intercepted or a loose ball is recovered by an opponent. The players *must* cover their men as soon as possible and prevent the offense from moving to the front court and an easy shot. There is also practice on the jump-ball transition in the offensive foul circle area. If the opponents get the tip, each player gets to his man as soon as possible.

After the defense gains possession of the ball, the offense scores, or the whistle blows, the players set up another transition possibility. The offense uses every possible type of offensive attack that the opponents may use. With the constant repetition of this drill, the defensive players get the necessary experience in practice which will be needed in regular games. It eventually becomes second nature for them to go on the defense as soon as the ball changes hands. A habit well formed becomes an immediate reflex action in a game; *drills are necessary*. Only through *repetition* can you hope to get immediate action. This is especially true when you are dealing with the defense. The immediate change from defense to offense can usually be attained much easier. It is only natural that the adrenaline pumps faster in most players when they go on the offensive.

The smooth changing of defenses while applying pressure on the ball can be very confusing to opponents. There were times during a game when I missed the key for one reason or another and wasn't sure what defense we were in until three or four passes were made in the front court. If the players can make it difficult for their defensive coach to know what they are doing when he misses the key, they certainly should be giving their opponents some problems. The longer the players hold off moving into the defense they will be playing when the opponents start passing the ball in the offensive lane, the more confusing the defense can be.

If the coach can miss the key, then it is natural to assume that a player may also miss it. This does happen at times, but the defense seldom gives up an easy field goal. When it does happen, the defensive man who missed the key usually was supposed to be guarding the basket area or an offensive man that happened to be positioned in the same area. Also, the players are schooled to talk to one another and any mix-up in the defense is usually corrected immediately. There have been times when the defense's slowness in correcting the mix-up only caused more confusion for the offense. A three-player zone and a two-player man-to-man can be confusing if the basket area is protected.

KEYS IN A MULTIPLE DEFENSE

In my first edition of the Amoeba defense, I mentioned that we used all types of keys to determine what defense we would eventually be using when the opponents would get to the offensive lane. I did not divulge the exact keys that we used. Naturally, I got quite a few inquiries about those keys.

Several years ago, I was talking to a coach who had been at West Virginia University in the early seventies. During the conversation, he told me that he and another assistant would scout three or four of Pitt's games every year to try and figure out the key we used in going from man to zone as the opponent was preparing to go into its front court offense. He said: "We never did figure out what it was." When I told him the key we used most of the time during that period, he said "How the hell could we have missed it?" Here's what the key was: when we were able to get back to our defensive end of the court before they got the ball to the center line, our number 1 defensive player guarding the man with the ball (usually the point guard) would turn and face his man before crossing the center line. This move told our players we would play man-to-man defense. If he did not turn and face his man until he got into the front court, we played zone, once inside the time hash marks. It was a very simple key for our players to understand and use efficiently, but it was evidently difficult for opponents to figure out.

The point that I am making with this story is that the simplest key can be confusing for the opponents in a multiple defense. Basketball is a game of constant motion. If your players execute the changes from one type of defense to another smoothly, it is difficult for the opponents to figure out the key quickly or easily. Many coaches who are using a multiple defense today are making most of their changes with a signal from the bench. Signaling may be the best way for some coaches. There were certain situations that required us to make a change by a command from the bench. However, I never liked the idea of players looking to the bench to see what they were going to do next, so most of our changes were made by the use of keys. Besides, it is very difficult for a coach to make the "live ball" changes with signals. The big thing is to make sure that the keys are not too complicated. The point is to confuse the opponents, not your own players. From time to time, you may have to change some of the keys. Do not do this too often or it *will* result in the confusion of your own players. Even when opponents have figured out the keys, a multiple defense, changing smoothly from one defense to another, is more effective in most cases than playing only a conventional defense.

Listed below are a few of the many keys we used to go from man to zone or vice-versa from 1965 to 1980.

Full and Three-Quarter Pressing Defenses

Dead Ball Keys—Back Court

1. Field goal made—man press to zone in offensive lane.
2. Foul made—1-2-2-1 zone press to man in offensive lane.
3. Any end court inbound pass—man press to zone in offensive lane.
4. Right side inbound pass (right of defense)—man press to zone in offensive lane.
5. Left side inbound pass—man press and also man defense in offensive lane.
6. "On the Ball" inbound pass—1-2-1-1 zone or man press to man or zone in offensive lane.
7. "Double Team" inbound pass—man press to zone in offensive lane.
8. "Centerfield" inbound pass—ideal for the 2-2-1 three-quarter zone press to man or zone in offensive lane.

9. Field goal made by certain player. Special keys for a certain game or games.
10. Foul made by certain player. Special keys for a certain game or games.
11. Field goal made on fastbreak—another special key—ideal for full court press to man or zone.

Live Ball Keys—Back Court

1. Double team—man to zone press if 1 defensive player double teams in corner; if not, stay in the man press (p. 187).
2. Clear-Out Offense—the 1-4 press offense keys more double teams in the backcourt (p. 164).
3. Missed field goals and fouls or turnovers keyed either a half-court press or offensive lane defense—man or zone. The Amoeba defense always tried to be on the ball at the center line.

NOTE: The live ball change from a pressing man defense to an offensive lane zone defense or vice-versa only takes place after the initial offensive thrust to the basket is stopped. Examples: when the ball is passed or dribbled away from the basket toward the backcourt or center line, or when the point guard signals, stands still or dribbles in place indicating for his team to set up their planned lane offense.

Half-Court Pressing Defenses

Dead Ball Keys—Front Court (Where Defense Starts)

1. Field goals made—trap press to offensive lane zone.
2. Fouls made—man press to offensive lane zone.
3. Right side inbound pass—man press to zone.
4. Left side inbound pass—man press all the way.
5. Baseline inbound pass—zone to man press or trap.

Live Ball Keys

1. Double team—man to zone (p. 150, 151, 168).
2. Position of number 1 defensive player—man to zone (p. 201).

Offensive Lane Defenses

Dead Ball Keys

Same as in the pressing defenses.

Offensive Lane

Live Ball Keys

1. Double team—(pp. 150, 151).
2. Position of 1 defensive player—(p. 201).
3. Pass from B to C area—(p. 195).
4. Point guard pass and follow—(p. 166).
5. Point guard pass and go away—(p.166).
6. Second Cycle of a continuity offense—(p. 162).
7. Clear out offense—(p. 164).
8. Point guard initial pass to left of defense—(p. 167).
9. Point guard initial pass to right of defense—(p. 167).

NOTE: The opportunity for the offense to score is minimized if there is pressure on the ball and the basket is protected by the weak-side defense during a "live ball" defensive change in the offensive lane.

Naturally you do not need all these keys to have an effective multiple defense. If the players are schooled well in the basic fundamentals of both man-to-man and zone defenses and if they know the how and when to use the jump-switch, fake jump-switch and double team, you could have a good multiple defense by using a minimum number of keys. Here is an example:

Pressing Defenses

Dead Ball Keys

1. "On the ball" inbound pass
2. "Double team" inbound pass
3. "Centerfield" inbound pass
4. Right side inbound pass

NOTE: Use these same keys also for the front court "dead ball" situations.

Live Ball Key

1. Double team

Offensive Lane Defenses

Dead Ball Key

1. Baseline inbound pass

Live Ball Keys

    1. Position of number 1 defensive player.
    2. Initial pass to right or left side of defense.

These are all simple keys and not difficult for the players to learn.

> *NOTE:* The "live ball" changes in the Amoeba are explained on pages indicated.

GRADING SYSTEM

Coach Ridl, during his tenure at Westminster and Pitt, used a grading system that gave credit for good defensive play. This grading system proved to be an accurate evaluation of the player's all around play in each game. Sometimes a player who had a great defensive game had a higher grade than a player who had scored from eighteen to twenty-five points. This type of incentive encourages good defensive play.

The grading method use was as follows:

Field goal attempt	− ¾	Offense rebound	+ 1
Field goal made	+ 2	Assist	+ 1
Foul made	+ 1	Blocked shot	+
Foul missed	− 1	Deflection	+ ½
Defense rebound	+ ½	Recovery	+ 2
		Turnover	− 2

NOTE: Players had to shoot over 40 percent from the field to get a + grade on shooting. Any deflection of a pass whether recovered or not was credited with a + ½.

Below is an actual record chart of a game played against Penn State.

Name	FGA FGM	FTA FTM	Rebs D-O	A	Bl	De	R	L	Gr	Time Pl
Shrews	1-5	3-6	3-1	8	0	2	3	2	+11½	33:00
Harris	10-15	5-6	4-1	2	0	3	1	2	+17½	32:30
Kelly	2-5	0-0	1-3	0	2	7	0	1	+6	19:20
Williams	6-12	0-0	0-4	1	0	5	1	1	+10½	21:35

Name	FGA FGM	FTA FTM	Rebs D-O	A	Bl	De	R	L	Gr	Time Pl
Richards	4-6	0-0	2-0	3	0	1	9	1	+24	39:45
Boyd	2-3	1-3	0-0	1	0	3	1	1	+7	13:40
T. Knight	1-5	0-0	1-1	0	0	1	2	0	+4	11:15
Strickland	0-4	0-0	0-0	3	0	2	1	3	−3	8:00
McClelland	1-3	0-0	3-0	0	1	5	0	0	+5	18:10
Haygood	0-3	2-2	0-1	0	0	0	0	0	+1	4:00
								Team 4		

I should point out that Richards, who had only eight points, had a better *grade* than Harris, who scored twenty-five points. This grading method gives a fairly good indication of the all-around play of each player.

SUMMARY

The Amoeba defense is designed to keep the type of defense used hidden as long as possible or at least until the ball is about to enter the offensive lane area. The defense may also change while the offense is moving within the offensive lane area.

This is accomplished by using the jump-switch, fake jump-switch and double team in both the man-to-man and zone defense. How and when the players make this change from one defense to the other is determined by pre-assigned *keys*, the defensive moves of certain players, or a pass from one certain area to another certain area within the offensive lane, etc.

CONCLUSION

You can see the importance of the jump-switch in the defenses you have studied in this book. The proper use of this defensive move can give your defense a "new look." If your players have a positive attitude toward learning to play the defense, it can be mastered in a much shorter time than you may think. This defense has proven its worth in the years we have used it. Many high school and college teams are already using variations of this type of multiple defense. The 1980s will see this type of defense become more popular than ever. This is one way, I am certain, to keep pace with the ever-improving offense.

PART III:
TEACHING, SPECIAL DRILLS AND RULES

10

Teaching the Amoeba

Bob Hill, a capable young assistant coach who worked with me for two years at the University of Pittsburgh and is now an assistant coach at the University of Kansas, put together a fine notebook for the players on the Amoeba defense. It was such a good notebook on the defense that I thought it was worthwhile to put it in this book. I made a number of changes when I edited it, but here it is in its entirety. Bob had only been with us one year when he put this notebook together. In that short period, he certainly was able to grasp a good understanding of the defense.

INTRODUCTION

The purpose of this notebook is to give you some early insight into our defense here at Pitt. It is our intention to bring you along slowly so that you will receive a sound understanding of the entire defense. You will receive a mailing once every week or two. The notebook you have been sent is for holding the information. You will be responsible for everything you receive from now until school starts.

NUMBERS OF PLAYERS IN FULL COURT MAN-TO-MAN AND WHY THEY HAVE NUMBERS

You will receive your defensive assignment prior to each game. At that time each player should know the opponents' full court offense. There will be adjustments many times prior to the game and during the game. Important things to remember about the full court man-to-man are:

1. There is *always* pressure on the ball.
2. The basket is *always* covered.
3. The players off the ball are *always* in a ball-you-man position or triangle.

The success of this defense will be determined by how well each man can play each position. You may have to play them *all* in the course of a game!

Each position is numbered, from 1 thru 5. Most of the time our 1 man will take the opponent's best ballhandler. Our 2 man will match with their second guard. Our 3 man is (most of the time) our quick forward, who will be assigned to whatever forward they use to break the presses. Our 4 man will match up with their power forward. Player 5 in our defense will be our center and will be assigned to their center.

Each player has a number because each position has a different responsibility. You will understand these responsibilities better as you read on.

RESPONSIBILITIES OF EACH MAN IN THE FULL COURT MAN-TO-MAN

Player 1 has to do his best to keep the ball from the opponent's best ballhandler. If 1's man does get the ball, despite 100 percent effort, his next job is to apply as much pressure while forcing him in the direction of 2 *(Diagram 10-1)* or the next closest defensive man. We have a standing rule which applies every game! We DO NOT allow any opposing player to dribble down the 12 foot extended *A* area in the middle of the floor (see *Diagram 10-1*).

On a jump-switch, 1 picks up the next open man down court. If he can't find one down the court, he heads for the no-ball area to look for one! Player 1 double-teams only at locations on the court where he is instructed to! (We will go into this more, later.)

Our 2 man will initiate jump-switches quite frequently *(Diagram 10-1)*. He must maintain "ball-you-man" position and jump-switch when he is as close as possible to the man with the

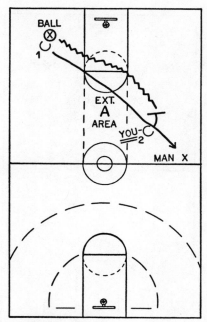

Diagram 10-1
Player 2 is in Ball-You-Man.
- Alert Stance
- Jump-Switch
- Fake Jump-Switch
- Double Team

ball. Usually, the only time you jump-switch is when the ball is being pushed in your direction or is coming at you! Sometimes 2 may jump-switch or double-team when the dribbler turns his back on him near the center or sidelines, but only when 2 is on the *strong side* of the court. After jump-switching successfully a time or two, the "fake jump-switch" will become effective and should be used. The man initiating the jump-switch will signal his teammates to trigger the movement. (We'll get into this more, later.)

In our full court man-to-man 3 *MUST* keep his head up and stay in position (ball-you-man) prepared to jump-switch, double-team or rotate at any time. (The success of this full court play depends on 3, 4, and 5 maintaining proper positioning and

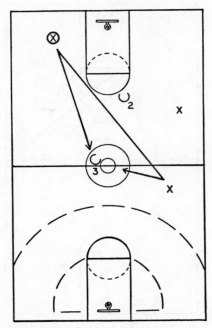

Diagram 10-2
- Alert Stance
- Cut Off Diagonal Cut
- Rotate
- Look for Lob or Long Pass.
Player 3 is in Ball-You-Man.

staying alert. *Each player must know where the ball is at all times* (Diagram 10-2)!

As 3, you must keep your man from the ball; look for the long pass or the lob; be prepared to umbrella when you are not part of a double team.

Our 4 man has the same responsibilities as 3 (*Diagram 10-3*). The key is to stay in position and be alert. When we are two or three passes away from the ball we *always* stay in a defensive stance ready to move. This goes for *ALL FIVE MEN*.

Player 5's responsibilities are not like those of his teammates (*Diagram 10-4*). In the second paragraph on the first page you learned that one of the things to remember about our full court defense is that we must *cover the basket*. That is 5's

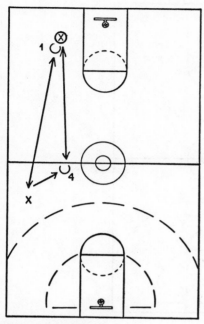

Diagram 10-3
Player 4 is in Ball-You-Man.
(Same responsibilities
as Player 3.)

Diagram 10-4

TOP PRIORITY. You must protect the basket 100 percent of the time or the efforts of your teammates will be of *no* use to us! Player 5 must stay in position, down in a defensive stance. Player 5 tries to steal a pass only when he is *positive* that a teammate is able to cover the basket or become 5. (You'll understand that better later.) Playing the 5 position includes looking for the lob or long pass; and umbrella whenever necessary. Umbrella is illustrated in *Diagram 10-5.*

YOUR NUMBER CAN CHANGE—
ACCORDING TO WHERE YOU ARE ON THE FLOOR

This defense has proven to be extremely effective and highly successful. This is why when a team plays against us a second time they are prepared with an idea to counter the pres-

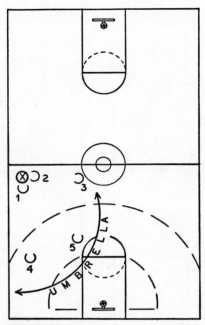

Diagram 10-5
This gives you an idea of what we
mean when we say *umbrella*.

sure. According to our experience, teams will sometimes have
their big men bring the ball down the floor! To respond to *that,*
our guards will go down court, clearing out, forcing *our* big men
to play 1, 2, and 3 in the full court man-to-man. Now you know
why *everyone on the team needs to know each position, making
the defense 100 percent foolproof!*

In order to give you really good examples of what we mean,
check *Diagrams 10-6* and *10-7. Diagram 10-6* shows you the
look Notre Dame gave us last season. Dantley brought the ball
up court and the rest of the floor was spread. *Diagram 10-7*
shows you how Marquette set up to break our defense. Against
both Notre Dame and Marquette, forwards brought the ball up
court. They did this because we were giving their guards a lot of
problems.

We must be ready to make adjustments *on the floor during
the game,* without taking a time out for every new look. If our

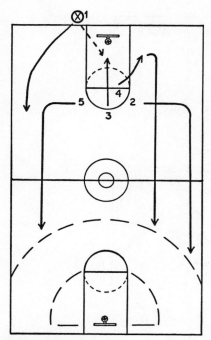

Diagram 10-6

Notre Dame cleared out for player 3—Dantley—to bring the ball up.

1 — Martin, 6'1"
2 — Williams, 6'1"
3 — Dantley, 6'6"
4 — Paterals, 6'3"
5 — Lambien, 6'11"

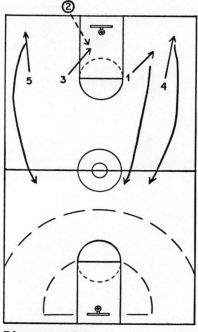

Diagram 10-7

Marquette cleared out for small forward, Tatum.

1 — Walton, 6'3"
2 — Lee, 6'1"
3 — Tatum, 6'7"
4 — Whitehead, 6'10"
5 — Ellis, 6'9"

scouting report shows us that the opponent's center takes the ball out-of-bounds, but the small forward takes it out when the game is underway, we have to adjust. For example, if their small forward takes it out and their center brings it down, then our big people must know the rules and responsibilities of 1 and 2. At the same time, our guards must adapt to the rules and responsibilities of 4 and 5.

Another example can be found where there is an early jump-switch and a complete rotation takes place. That *could*

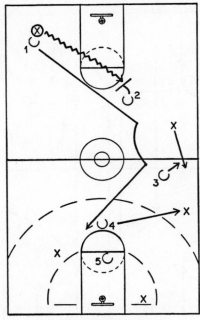

Diagram 10-8

leave *1* in *4's position* ... (*Diagram 10-8*). Anytime there is a rotation, chances are your responsibility will change, no matter what position you started in at the beginning of the series. From the examples given, you can imagine the various combinations teams throw at us. As a player you need to know the responsibilities of each position. The key is to keep pressure on the ball and the basket protected. If we do those things, then we'll be OK.

Here is an explanation of the jump-switches, fake jump-switches and double teams. We use the jump-switch for six reasons:

a. Apply as much pressure on the ball as possible
b. Wear the opponent down
c. Force the opponent into turnovers without hand-checking
d. Collect as many steals as possible
e. Aid us in controlling the momentum of the game
f. Set up the ideal double team situation

The success of a jump-switch is determined by:

a. Pressure on the ball
b. Pushing the dribbler toward closest teammate
c. Position of teammates
d. Timing of jump-switch

TERMINOLOGY

Jump-Switch

This movement is used when the ball is being forced in your direction . . . *you* must initiate the jump-switch by yelling "GO" and jumping, under control, out in front of the man dribbling the ball. The man who initially was guarding the ball either takes your man or the next open man as he pivots down court. Or, he may double-team.

Ball-You-Man

This term refers to your positioning off the ball (when you are *not* guarding the man with the ball). You should be able to see the ball and your man by using peripheral vision. (In other words, you don't have to turn your head either way.)

Umbrella

This movement is used only, but always, when there is a double team. After the double team takes place, the other three players surround the double team in an umbrella fashion. *NOT* right on top of the double team, but at a comfortable distance, encouraging a lob or long pass *OVER* the umbrella. (We must pick off those passes.)

Rotation

This move takes place when a jump-switch is executed. The position of the jump-switch will determine how much everyone rotates. If 2 initiates a jump-switch with 1, 1 either pivots down court and picks up 2's man *or* takes the next open man. If 3 thinks he should rotate and cover 2's man, then 1 may pick up 3's man. If not, 3's man then may be 4's and so on. If you can't find a man, you go to the basket; then look for the open man.

Dead Ball

Any time the man you are guarding is dribbling the ball and he picks up his dribble . . . you immediately *yell* "dead ball" and get right in his face. Again your feet are stationary, shoulder-width, and your hands follow the ball.

Fake Jump-Switch

It is exactly what it sounds like. It works after a successful jump-switch or two. When the ball is being pushed toward the man about to execute the fake, he will make a quick sharp move toward the ball and then get back. This may cause the ball handler to pick up his dribble; it may cause him to reverse his dribble; he may try to make a quick pass. That means the man faking the jump-switch must be alert for anything.

The Double Team

This will be used primarily on certain areas of the floor *(Diagram 10-9)*. Once again, we must use proper footwork and hand work in order to execute an effective double team. Anytime we double-team, we'll do it by using a shoulder-width stance and *holding that stance*. Our arms and hands will follow the ball and *won't be used to reach!!* The purpose of our double team is to force a long or lob pass or create the five-second call leading to a possible turnover *(Diagram 10-10)*. There is no easier way for an offense to create the "give and go" than by breaking a double team. Notice the correct position of the feet on the double team. You must make it impossible for the player with the ball to break through the trap.

The timing of moves like the jump-switch and double team is extremely vital to the effectiveness of the overall defense. The jump-switch must be executed close and quick. If it's done loosely, then the jump-switch will work *against us*. A double team must be executed after reading the situation and the floor. (Example: If a man picks up his dribble as the result of a jump-switch at half court, it's an ideal situation for a double team,

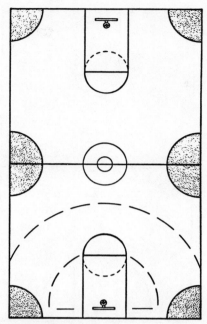

Diagram 10-9

We double-team anywhere on the court, with the right opportunity. What you see here are the *ideal* areas—because of the lines on the court. Out-of-bounds lines are on your side during a double team.

which should be executed immediately.) You can't leave your man to double-team if it's cross-court or any unreasonable distance. Keep it close and quick.

AREAS OF THE FLOOR
WHERE WE WANT TO DOUBLE-TEAM,
AND WHO DETERMINES IT

Again, this topic has been covered and you should have a good idea of what is expected of you. *Diagrams 10-9* and *10-10* show you *where* to double-team and how. You'd better know this!! We encourage the double team anywhere on the floor, if the

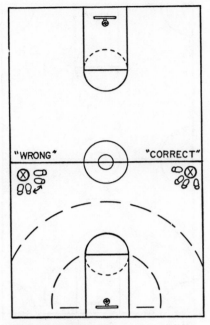

Diagram 10-10

"Wrong"

• Stance too narrow.

• Gap between defensive players.

"Correct"

• Shoulder-width stance.

• Inside feet together.

Hands follow the ball.

situation is right. What makes the situation right? The most obvious one is after a properly executed jump-switch takes place and the ballhandler picks up his dribble. This is a prime situation and must be *read*.

Another situation is when the opponent clears out, letting one man bring the ball up by himself. This is what we want them to do. With patience, the man guarding the ball pushes his man in the direction of his teammate, still in the back court. Now your question is, why is there still another guy in the back court? That brings us to a golden rule within our full court man-to-man defense: *If you are the last man to cross the half*

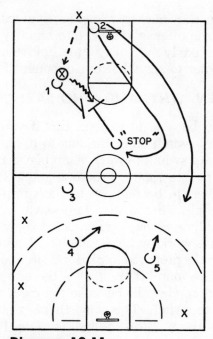

Diagram 10-11

A good time to double-team on a clear-out.

court line on a clear out, you stay (Diagram 10-11)! This means that we are going to play 2-on-1 in the back court and 3-on-4 in the front court. Understand? This is why it's so important for *everyone* to stay in *position* all of the time. When this occurs, the double team situation could very easily present itself. You'll understand this better as time goes on.

WHEN AND WHY WE FAKE JUMP-SWITCH

When you try something a lot, your opponent is going to learn how to play against it, sooner or later. Therefore, you must respond with a move to make your opponent play you honestly. Our goal is to jump-switch as much as possible, not allowing things to get out of control. A fake jump-switch is used to keep the offense on their toes and alert. Following a successful jump-switch or two, it's good to take one to see how the offense responds. The ballhandler may pick up his dribble, he may reverse his dribble, they may try a loop . . . at any rate, if the fake is done correctly, the offense *will have to react*. We may use fake jump-switches early in the game before actually jump-switching, in order to see what our opponent is going to do.

WHEN, WHY, AND WHO SAYS "GO"

You should be able to explain this if you are doing your work! In a jump-switch someone has to initiate the action. In order for the jump-switch to work, each player has to do his job. When all five people rotate, everyone must stay alert and in position. However, to best illustrate the jump-switch, we will use only two people. First of all, a jump-switch *can* take place at any spot on the floor, *if* the conditions are right. If the defensive man on the ball is working hard and doing his job, then the man off the ball can stay prepared to read the situation and create the jump-switch. The man off the ball is the one who yells "GO," creating the action. He yells because the man on the ball needs to know when to switch. This way, there is no question about when and what the man on the ball is to do. If the situation is right for a double team, 1 stays on the man with the ball and you have the double team.

RESPONSIBILITIES OF 3, 4, AND 5 ON A DOUBLE TEAM BY 1 AND 2

If 1 and 2 double-team, then the other guys *umbrella*. It doesn't matter who double-teams, the others must umbrella, or the double team won't work (*Diagram 10-12*). When 3, 4 and 5 see the double team, they move into position, leaving their men and splitting the distance between the double team and their men. This encourages the lob pass. After the umbrella is formed, if *your* man penetrates the umbrella *you must take him*. We'll get into this more when practice begins. (Just understand this information for now).

BALL-YOU-MAN PRINCIPLES IN FULL COURT MAN-TO-MAN

This has been covered once before but is *vital* to the success of our defense. Each player *must* be in position all of the

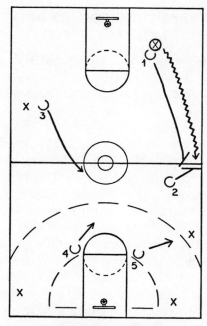

Diagram 10-12

time, ready to jump-switch, fake jump-switch, double-team, rotate, cut off his man, intercept lob passes or umbrella! If even
one player breaks down, then the entire defense breaks down.

Ball-you-man principles were probably used on teams
you've played on. However, I doubt if you were ever responsible
for as many things within your defense. Therefore, it was easy
for you to relax and not be as alert as maybe you should have
been. *And* you got away with it!! No longer! You will be responsible for too many things *off the ball. That is the key to any solid
man-to-man defense.* You will need to get to your man the *second* we score or turn the ball over. In college ball, if one of us is
slow getting to his man, our opponents release that man for
lay-ins. You must get to your man and then stay alert and in
position.

In the simplest terms, ball-you-man position means you
can see your man *and* the ball *ALL OF THE TIME.*

How quick you are compared to how quick your man is will
determine exactly how far off your man you will be able to play.

WHAT KEYS EVERYONE TO DROP BACK
INTO THE ZONE?

This zone is called "31." It is unlike all other zones and more suitable for a multiple-type defense. The players here at Pitt believe in it and have developed great pride in playing it over the last few years.

There is no specific answer to the question above. Last season, we keyed the zone various ways. As you'll experience when we begin to play the games on our schedule, we'll be extremely prepared for each contest. Therefore, we might stay man-to-man until our opponent makes the initial pass to begin their offense. That pass *might* key the zone. There may be times when we won't fall into the zone until the ball is passed to a specific area on the floor or maybe to a specific player. Nearly anything *could* key us dropping back into the zone or "31." The coaching staff will make it as simple as possible for you to understand by preparing each player for every game. When the key says to go zone, we usually don't go into it until the ball penetrates the front court "hash marks" *(Diagram 10-13)*. Once we drop to the zone or "31" there are situations that call for us to go back to man-to-man. *We'll* get more into that later.

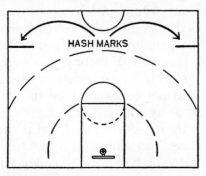

Diagram 10-13
Play past this area could key us to
drop back into the zone or "31."

ZONE THAT'S DIFFERENT—
BASIC FORMATION OF THE ZONE

If you were to talk to opposing coaches or fans, they may tell you that our defense looks like a 1-3-1 or 1-2-2 or they may not be sure. In essence, it's a 1-1-2-1 that becomes almost *anything* following a pass or movement by the offense. To make it simple for you to comprehend we'll discuss the specific areas within the zone. There are six (6) areas for everyone to be aware of! There are two (2) "C" areas; two (2) "B" areas; one (1) "A" area; and a "no-ball area." Each player must understand this before he can clearly understand the responsibilities of each man (*Diagram 10-14*).

Each man has a number. Obviously, they are numbered one through five. Players 1 and 2 have similar responsibilities all the time, 3 and 4 have the same responsibilities, and 5 has his own job. Therefore, each man within the zone is playing his own game, but together with everyone else. Check *Diagram 10-15* for the basic set.

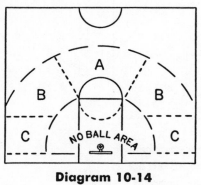

Diagram 10-14

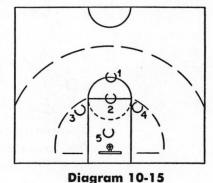

Diagram 10-15

RULES AND GENERAL INFORMATION WITHIN THE ZONE

The two most important rules within this zone: (1) there is pressure on the ball; (2) the basket is protected 100 percent of the time. If we stick to these rules, then the zone will be effective. As the season goes on, you will see how some of the rules may be adjusted to different situations. One rule will always prevail—the low post will always be fronted. Not always true at the high post. This zone has been designed to *force* the offense to make *very good passes* to be successful. We believe that passing is one aspect of the game where many players and teams aren't real proficient. Therefore, if we pressure the ball, protect the hoop, the posts and front, it's going to take very good passes to beat us. The percentage is in *our* favor.

It's very important for you to understand the way the floor is divided into six areas. Those areas will be referred to every day throughout the year.

One rule that holds true within the zone as well as the man-to-man has to do with our double team procedure. Any time we double-team (it doesn't matter who double-teams), the other three players *umbrella*. (We got the double team on the baseline most of the time last year.) If you are in the umbrella and one of the opponents breaks to the ball from your area of the floor, you must take him *(Diagram 10-16)*.

Diagram 10-16
This shows what happens when we "give" the baseline to create a double team with an umbrella.

When the other team is taking the ball out under the basket, the 5 man will always be guarding the man taking the ball out. He will angle to protect the hoop. If there is a pass to the corner, and the man catching the pass is a *guard* or *not a big man*, then we will double-team with the 5 man and one of our guards, either 1 or 2 *(Diagram 10-17)*. If the man catching the ball is a big forward or the center, we will never double-team. If this happens, then 5 will cover the man alone *(Diagram 10-18)*.

Footwork is important in some of the coverages within the zone. If you are playing either 3 or 4, and there is a pass to your side (in the B Area), you must attack the ball with your inside foot up and inside arm up. You are encouraging a pass to the

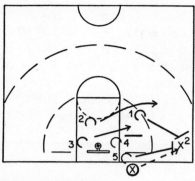

Diagram 10-17

This shows the *double team* in the corner, following inbounds pass to X². X² must be a smaller player. The other three players umbrella.

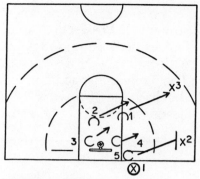

Diagram 10-18

This shows that, when X² is a larger player, normal coverage is used.

corner and protecting the no-ball area (*Diagram 10-19*). If the pass is made to the corner, your job is to drop to the low post and front the low post or medium post area. If you have your feet in proper position, then you will be able to drop to the block a lot quicker (*Diagram 10-20*)!

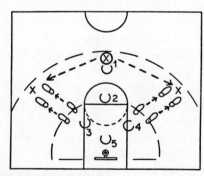

Diagram 10-19

This shows the footwork you are to use to force pass to corner (3 and 4).

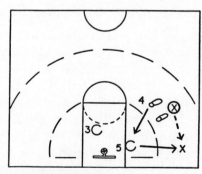

Diagram 10-20

This shows why it's necessary to maintain proper footwork on a pass to the corner. In this case, player 4 has his left foot forward and his right foot back—it's easy for 4 to slide to the block without changing his feet.

If you are playing the 5 position and there is a pass from strong side *B* Area to *C* Area, that man is *YOUR RESPONSIBILITY!* If he is going to take the shot, you are permitted to go up with him, giving the appearance of an attempted blocked shot. The 5 man must go up with the shooter, on the *inside* away from the baseline *(Diagram 10-21)*. Once the five man lands, he heads for the other end and a fast break lay-up *(Diagram 10-22)*.

Diagram 10-21

Very important:
When the man in the corner shoots, player 5 can take a "flyer" at the ball, but to the inside of the court!

Diagram 10-22

Player 5 stays to the inside, then releases for the fast break.

It is necessary that each player keep his arms up while we are in the zone. Extended arms will make it appear much harder to penetrate, which is a plus for us.

When the ball is in the *B* Area, with 3 and 2 on the ball, 1 plays the high post. He fronts the high post when the ball is in the *B* Area *(Diagram 10-23)*. However, if it goes to the *C* Area, then he will front the high post with a closed stance from top side with right arm extended. He uses this defensive stand to keep from being screened off by the high postman on a diagonal pass from *C* to weak side *A* or *B* area *(Diagram 10-24)*.

When you have low post responsibility and there is *no one* in the low post, you then move up to the midpost area *(Diagram 10-25)*. Players 3, 4, or 5 may have this responsibility. If you are in the midpost area and someone breaks to the low post, your teammates must alert you so that you can front him.

That takes us to the rule of the weak side man when the

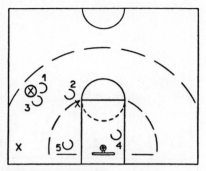

Diagram 10-23

Player 2 fronts the high-post man, when the ball is in the "B" area and player 2 has high-post responsibility.

Diagram 10-24

This shows how player 2 fronts the high-post man, when the ball is in the "C" area.

• Topside closed stance.

Diagram 10-25

This shows the ball in "B" area and no one in the low post. If X^4 broke low, player 4 would have to alert player 5 to front him.

strong side low *and* high post are vacant. If X^5 cuts to the low post, then 4 merely tells 5 to front him (*Diagram 10-26*). If X^4 cuts to the high post, 4 could alert 1, and with 1 playing it according to where the ball is. (If the ball is in the *B* Area, he fronts him facing the ball. If the ball is in the *C* Area, then he uses a closed stance topside. See *Diagram 10-27*. Now let's deal with the weak side man when the low post is taken and the high

Diagram 10-26

This shows the coverage on a weak-side cut to the strong-side low post. Player 4 must alert player 5 to front the low post.

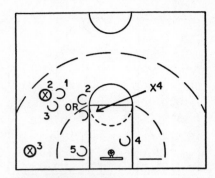

Diagram 10-27

This shows how player 2 covers the high post when X⁴ makes weak-side cut—ball is in either "B" or "C" area.

post is vacant (*Diagram 10-28*). That leaves one offensive man weak side with 4. Player 2 is free to "cheat" toward passing lane away from X¹ and X². Player 2 can often get a steal on this move. If X⁴ cuts to the high post, 4 will alert 2, who plays it accordingly (*Diagram 10-29*). The coverages will vary according to where the ball is. Each player must read the various situations. We could go on here; however, I think this will give you enough to think about.

Diagram 10-28

This shows the low post in use and the high post vacant. Player 5 fronts the low post.

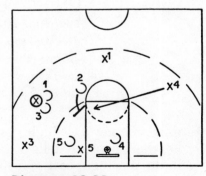

Diagram 10-29

This shows X⁴ moving from weak side to vacant high post. Player 2 must take him.

WHY THE ZONE AND TOTAL DEFENSE IS SO EFFECTIVE

The big reason for our defensive success is that *everyone believes in it!* It has been very effective for a long time. With hard work it will continue to be successful. It takes a lot of concentration from everyone, including the coaching staff!! This defense kept our team in a lot of games last season, which, on paper, we should have not been in. Therefore, we should be even better this season.

Because of team quickness we may do *more* things this season. So be prepared to learn and work hard.

YOU ARE RESPONSIBLE FOR THIS ENTIRE NOTEBOOK!!

The Coaching Staff

11

Drills on Special Defensive Skills

Drills are necessary to perfect good defensive fundamentals. Many defensive drills have already been illustrated in this book. Those drills pertained to the material explained in each chapter.

Following are some drills on special defensive skills that will help in developing the overall strength of any defense. *Diagram 11-1* involves two skills that are important to anyone who desires to be a good defensive player. Both these skills are neglected by most players in a game if they do not practice them. The repetition of a drill in practice will eventually automatically carry over into the game when the need for the skill arises.

DEFENSIVE RECOVERY DRILLS

The coach passes the ball from *A* area to a player in *B* area. The defensive player guarding the player "one pass away" is using the proper closed stance with the right hand extended between the ball and his man; the arm is rotated in the proper way so his thumb is down and the palm is facing the passer. The coach makes his pass in such a way that permits the defensive player to slap the ball toward his own basket with his right hand. Most players want to *open up* and hit it with their left hand or catch it. When a player tries to slap the pass with the left hand or catch it, he just naturally *opens up* to the ball, and this is a *poor* defensive move when the ball is one pass away. If the passer fakes his pass and the defensive player opens, which necessi-

Diagram 11-1

tates a forward movement, he becomes the victim of the *back door play*. *The rule should be that you never open up under these circumstances*. You can still catch the ball from a closed stance if the opportunity is there. Keeping the closed stance forces the player to learn to block the pass with the closest hand to the passer. With practice they can learn to intercept the pass this way as well as when they open up.

The second skill is now practiced by the other player who was supposed to receive the pass. After the interception, the player starts a *slow* dribble down court (does not protect his dribble). The other player comes up behind the dribbler and with an upper motion of his closest hand slaps the ball away from the dribbler and recovers it. This drill helps players to always remember that in the transition period, when they are going back on defense and are behind the dribbler (which happens often), they should always make an attempt to steal the ball in this manner. This is one of the easiest ways to make a *recovery*. The dribbler often forgets about the opponents behind him. Too many players pass up this golden opportunity during the course of a game. By using an upward motion of their arms, they can slap the ball away from the dribbler without fouling.

Another drill that teaches the defensive player to keep a closed stance and slap the pass with the hand closest to the ball is illustrated in *Diagrams 11-2* and *3*. The coach does not attempt to make a successful pass to X¹ so that the 1 defensive player may get to practice using his right hand to slap the ball to X² who returns it to the coach (*Diagram 11-2*). X¹ immediately goes back door as in *Diagram 11-3*. The defensive player stays

Diagram 11-2

Diagram 11-3

with him using a closed stance until X^1 moves into the foul lane area, where he opens up to the ball by pivoting on his left foot. X^1 keeps going back and forth at least four or five times and the defensive player keeps slapping the coach's pass. The defensive player also gets practice in opening up at the proper time in the foul lane area. The coach at times may also try to make a successful back door pass. He will sometimes fake the pass as X^1 moves out to receive the ball, and when X^1 goes backdoor, attempts a pass to him. This helps to teach the proper time to open up. This is also a good conditioning drill.

As I mentioned in Chapter 2, page 37, a good drill in teaching defensive players the proper footwork and positioning necessary in a good man-to-man defense is to run Dr. Carlson's figure eight. The offense, in an attempt to score, runs all the various options illustrated in *Diagrams 2-1* through *2-5*. This gives the defense good practice on how to play every position on and off the ball, the give and go, the back door cut, and the help and recover move. It also helps the player to perfect the slide and glide movement and the when and where to open up to the ball, two fundamentals that must be executed properly if a man-to-man defense is to be effective.

DEFENSING BASELINE DRIVE

Another skill that has become more important to learn is the proper method of playing the dribbler on his baseline drive. There was a time that no matter how you defensed this move, the defense player would nearly always be guilty of the foul

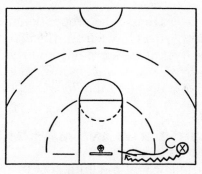

Diagram 11-4

when physical contact was made. In recent years the Rules
Committee has made a greater effort to emphasize the importance of the officials' placing more responsibility on the offensive
player when contact is made under these conditions. *Diagram
11-4* shows the defensive player keeping the offensive driver in
the four foot lane behind the basket. Then, as they near the
basket, he positions himself so that the offensive player must
throw himself into the defensive player in order to get on the
front side of the backboard to shoot. He sets himself in a stationary position with his arms high above his head.

Diagram 11-5 shows this same drill with a double team
from the defensive player on the weak side. When the driver is
beating his man, this can be a very successful defensive maneuver. The *Amoeba defense* uses this double team trap on the
baseline in its man-to-man just like it does in its zone. Notice
how 3, 4 and 5 are in the umbrella position. The only way you

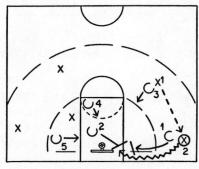

Diagram 11-5

can teach your players to use the proper defense without fouling on situations like this is to have drills in which they can practice doing it properly. Ten players are used on the double team drill as the driver tries to make a successful pass out of this double team and the players in the umbrella attempt to make the interception.

DEFENSING THE LOW AND MEDIUM POST AREA

Defensing the low and medium post in any defense should vary depending on the size and the ability of the post man and the location of the ball. When the ball is located in the *A* or high *B* area, an inside closed stance is required, as shown in *Diagram 11-6*. Defensive players 1 and 2 illustrate the proper positions. *Diagram 11-7* shows positions when the ball is located in the *B* or high *C* area. Notice that the 1 and 2 defensive players are playing in front or behind the postman. It is often best to play behind the postman when the ball is in the *B* or *C* area if you are overmatched in size or the postman has above average mobility. *Diagram 11-8* illustrates only one defensive position on the medium postman, but three different positions against the low postman when the ball is located in the *C* area. The closed stance should always be on the baseline side if the postman is *right handed*. If he is left handed it is best to use the inside position. It would be just the opposite on the *left* side of the *offensive* court.

When a pass is successful in the medium or low post area it is best to double-team the ball whenever possible. The closest

Diagram 11-6

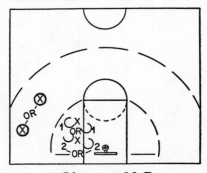

Diagram 11-7

Diagram 11-8

player to the ball has this responsibility. *Diagrams 11-9, 10 and 11* illustrate this double team. *Diagram 11* shows how the other three defensive players umbrella in an attempt to split the post-man's passing lanes.

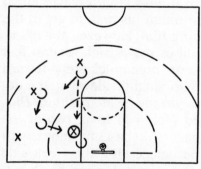

Diagram 11-9

Diagram 11-10

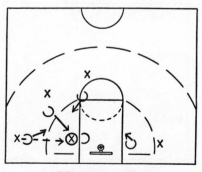

Diagram 11-11

Players can practice these defensive fundamentals by having a half court defensive drill against a five man offense that features medium and low post positioning. Any defense that stops the *power plays* and the *pass off* from these two positions is bound to be successful. Both the zone and man defenses in the Amoeba attempt to accomplish this end.

REBOUNDING WHEN FRONTING LOW-POST AREA

Some coaches hesitate to front a player in the low or medium post area, because in order to do so you must give up the good defensing rebounding position on an unsuccessful field goal attempt. This disadvantage can be minimized to a degree by having the defensive player fronting his man move quickly toward the baseline behind the backboard, and then move back out in an attempt to get good inside position. Most offensive players will be successful in checking a player out if the defensive player tries to fight through his man to get in the proper rebound position after fronting him. However, the offensive player often tends to stand still or move back several feet when checking out. By taking two or three quick steps toward the baseline and backboard and then sliding sideways, the defensive player has a good chance to get the inside position (*Diagram 11-12*). Both Larry Bird and Moses Malone, two of the better rebounders in the NBA, make this baseline move with great success. If this method is not successful, the weak side defensive player can cross over to the strong side and block out,

Diagram 11-12

Diagram 11-13

while the player fronting slides over the top and covers the area in front of the basket, as in *Diagram 13*.

DEFENSING OUT-OF-BOUNDS ON THE SIDE COURT

When applying pressure on an inbound pass from the sidecourt, the best chance for a successful recovery is when you prevent a *short* pass. This can be best accomplished if the 1 defensive player is given the responsibility to stop it. Regardless of what position he takes—*on the ball, double team* or *centerfield*—his primary duty is to prevent this short pass. *Diagram 11-14* shows 1 in all three positions. When he plays "on the ball" he positions himself in such a way to see as many offensive players as possible. In *Diagram 14* he is opened up enough that he can see all four opponents. He must pick up any player that comes within the imaginary ten foot radius as shown in the diagram. When he is double-teaming with 2, he immediately drops toward the "on-ball" position when 2's man moves to get out of the double team. If 1 is in the centerfield position, he picks up the first player to move in to receive the short inbound pass. If he is not successful in preventing this short pass and the receiver of the pass is within two or three feet of the out-of-bounds line, he can double-team with the teammate who is guarding the receiver. The double team near the sidelines gives the defense a second chance for a recovery. If unable to double-team, he must take his own man, who was the inbound passer. This must be practiced as a drill to do it properly during a game.

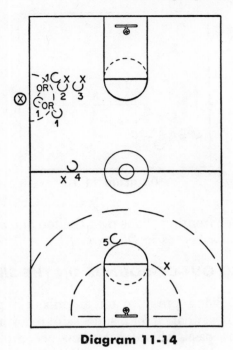

Diagram 11-14

CONCLUSION

The additional defensive skills in this chapter will help make any multiple defensive system that much more effective. During the preseason these drills should be a part of the regular defensive practice at least every other practice session. After the season begins once a week should be sufficient.

The author has attempted to organize this book to give the reader a complete understanding of a multiple defensive system as the answer to slowing up the ever-improving offenses in basketball today. Any coach who is willing to put in the time necessary to develop a multiple defensive system will find the effort well worthwhile.

12

The Rules?
Time for Some
Changes?

Certain key rule changes over the last fifty years have been partly responsible for making basketball the great game it is today. The rule change that was probably the most influential in making it a popular game was the elimination of the jump ball after every score in 1937. Since then, the game, with its constant motion and lightning-speed action performed by highly skilled athletes, has made the game a spectator's delight. However, these very characteristics have made the game, in the confined space in which it is played, a very difficult game to officiate. Perhaps it's time to take a good look at the rules to see if there are any changes that could be made to make the job of officiating the game a little easier. Yes, and to go one step further, changes that would make the game more fair for both players and coaches. We may find that the time has come when some adjustments or changes in the rules should be made. There is no question that in the area of the rules there is need for improvement. Many persons close to the game will agree with this premise. *Remember the saying "necessity is the mother of invention."*

It took a football coach to say something that has been evident for a long time. Bill Walsh, the head football coach of the San Francisco 49ers said in his article in *Sports Illustrated,* July 26, 1982, "In basketball the players are so good that they have gone beyond the rules." Is this condition really good for the game? When watching games in the NBA you see players traveling with the ball constantly without being called for the violation. This is especially true on the "dunk shot." You see a dribbler charging into a defensive player—putting *his knee into the other's chest* when going in for a lay-up or dunk—without the call being made! Should the interpretation of the rule be determined by the offensive skill of the players? It seems to me this is the way the game is going, at least in the NBA, and it is carrying over into the college game.

Now a move is being made in the college ranks to make changes in the rules that will take it several steps closer to the NBA basketball rules. The problem is that the individual conferences are making their own rules. They are changing two of the more basic rules that are naturally upsetting many officials and coaches. Several conferences from the Big East to the Pacific Coast have experimented with shot clocks of 30 to 45 seconds. Some will be turned on for the whole game. Some will be off in the closing minutes, and some will not start until the ball crosses midcourt. The other change is that a basket from nineteen feet or more—the top of the key—will count three points in six conferences. Three more conferences will have a three-point line ranging as far out as the Big Sky's twenty-one feet, three inches, but still well short of the 23-9 used in the NBA. These changes could be good for the game, but with all the different sets of rules it is only going to make the game more confusing for the officials, players, and spectators. *This has all happened because of the conservative nature of the National Rules Committee (NCAA).* If they are going to have a three-point line and a shot clock, it should be the same for all colleges and high schools. The rules committee should act on this immediately. I vote for the 30-second clock up to the last three minutes of the game, and the shot line at 21 feet from the *backboard,* which is at the top of the key. Only the best shooters have any consistency beyond 21 feet.

TWO OR THREE OFFICIALS

When the jump ball was eliminated after each score, the game moved at a much faster pace. It became evident that one official could not keep pace with the game. Gradually, the game began to use two officials. I remember distinctly one of the last games I officiated by myself. While I was stationed at Fort Benning, Georgia, in 1942 during World War II, the New York Celtics stopped at the fort to play a fine Paratroopers team. I was asked to officiate. It may have been the last year this great team played as a unit. As I recall, the only original Celtic still playing was Davey Banks. I can remember, as I was racing up and down the floor to stay close to the action, I thought it would not be long until two officials would be a standard procedure for basketball games at all levels. Yes, back then it was time to go to two officials.

Now, in the 1980s, there are quite a few major conferences and universities using three officials. Is this the answer to helping the officials? To date, the quality of officiating by three officials has not been impressive. The game can be better handled by two officials who get *into the game* and call everything they believe to be a violation. There must be primary and secondary duties for two officials to work well together, but I feel that two officials going into a game with the idea of calling everything believed to be a violation (as though each is the only official on the game) makes for the best officiated game. An official who gets upset when his partner makes a call not in his primary area is completely wrong.

It is very difficult for three officials to get into the game as they should. In the *confined space* where basketball is played, two officials can do the job if they are alert. When three officials are used, for one reason or another, one or two of them have a difficult time getting into the *flow* of the game.

The size of the basketball floor has a lot to do with the problem. When basketball went to two officials in the early 1940s, it was difficult for one official to keep up with the flow of the game. Two officials were needed. The length of the floor was too much for one official to stay close to the action during the continuous flow of play up and down the floor. The opposite is true when three officials are used. The size of the floor is *not large enough* for three officials to operate smoothly together. It almost seems as though they get in each other's way. Often, two officials close to the action and to each other hesitate to make the call. This causes the most obvious violations not to be called.

Since so many *judgment* calls have to be made in basketball, the angle of vision often determines what call is made. No official should be offended when his partner makes a call out of his territory. That's the reason why the game should use the two officials to *the fullest degree*. If an official calls *any violation* he sees, regardless of whether he is in the primary position or not, the game will be better.

The nature of the game and the rules makes this the only realistic viewpoint. Somehow the game has strayed away from this idea. It should not be considered poor officiating when both officials blow the whistle on a violation, differing on the call. A jump ball resolves this situation better than rewarding one team and penalizing the other. The most disheartening thing for a coach to hear from an official is: "I know, coach, but it wasn't my call." The statement has been heard by many coaches over the years. Neither the officials nor anyone else should be blamed for this trend of thinking, but it now dominates and it is wrong. With this type of thinking, in many ways, only *one* official is being used. The official should not worry about infringing upon his partner's territory when it comes to calling a violation. With two such officials, a well-officiated game is more likely to be the result.

Another good reason why basketball should have stayed with two officials at this time is that it is not economically feasible for most high schools and colleges to hire three officials. But since basketball has committed itself to using both the two and three official system, and since quantity does not necessarily mean quality, how may the official situation be improved?

The answer may be a changing or adjusting of the rules most difficult to call accurately. These rules are: (1) traveling; (2) charging and blocking; (3) screening; and (4) defensive goal tending.

TRAVELING

At this writing, the traveling rule in basketball is so haphazardly called that many players and some coaches, and yes, even a few officials don't know what traveling with the ball really is. The rules are very explicit about what constitutes traveling, but for one reason or another, it seems to be, along with the contact rule, the most difficult rule to call with consistency. Before I elaborate on the rules concerning traveling, a question arises that will not be answered in this chapter. What is taking place in the game of basketball, when the more skilled players in the pros are permitted to walk all over the place without being called for traveling; while in the lower levels, traveling is called over fifty percent of the time when a player lifts his pivot foot before releasing his pass? A high school player watching NBA play-off games might ask, "Are they playing by the same traveling rules I play by?" Many players do not know that lifting your pivot foot before you pass or shoot the ball is allowed. They do not know it because they have been called for traveling so often for lifting the pivot foot. In an informal survey of players, coaches, and officials concerning this rule, many players, and some coaches and officials said, "when a player lifts his pivot foot before releasing the *pass,* a traveling violation occurs." The rule is explicit: (Rule 4, Sec. 25, p. 31, items 3a & b—1980): "A ball handler is permitted to lift the pivot foot (if he does not drag it along the floor) as long as the ball leaves the hand before the pivot foot touches the floor again. The only time a player is *not allowed* to lift the pivot foot before the ball leaves the hand is on the *dribble.*"

On the other hand, traveling is *not* consistently called on the jump shot when a player uses the "one-two" motion (that is, after he has stopped his dribble or received a pass, he takes a step, moves the pivot foot even with the other foot, places it down on the floor, and then jumps in the air to take the shot). This move makes it easier to get more power and control in the jump shot. According to the rules, this is traveling and should be easy to call, but the violation is inconsistently called, causing many players to use this move frequently. Players also use this one-two motion on the "power play" under the basket. If the player does not drop the ball to the floor (one dribble) while taking the step, he is traveling. This one-two motion is also used illegally on many *dunk* shots. There is no question that "dunking" is one of the more spectacular plays in the game today. The crowd loves the "dunk." It's such a crowd-pleasing move that the officials get carried away with it themselves, often ignoring the violation. If officials are going to let players use the one-two motion to get the power for dunking the ball, the rule on traveling should be changed, conforming to the practice.

Although clearly stated, the first part of the rule on traveling (Rule 4, Sec. 25, p. 30) is difficult for officials to call accurately. In part, it states that if a player receives the ball in the air and lands on the floor with both feet at the same time, the player may then pivot with either foot. However, when the player comes down on one foot first and then on the other, he may only pivot on the foot that hit the floor *first*. It also states if the player alights on one foot, he may jump off the floor and alight with both feet simultaneously, but he may not pivot before releasing the ball. The rule continues in the same vein if he catches the ball with one foot off the floor. It seems to me that regardless of which of these ways the player comes down and stops, he should be allowed to pivot on either foot. What advantage has been gained by using the last alighting foot as the pivot foot? The rule should merely state that upon receiving the ball while moving, if the player has not violated the traveling rule by the time he has stopped, the player may use either foot when pivoting. In the quick action of the player, it is often impossible for an official to see accurately the exact footwork used when stopping after receiving the pass. Since the advantage is minimal, why should an official have to worry about which foot the player pivots on *after he has stopped*? This simpler rule would help the officials be more consistent and accurate in calling the traveling violation.

Another move that has caused confusion over the years occurs when a player from a standstill fakes a shot and then takes *a long step* and glides through the air past the defensive player for a lay-up or pass-off. Some players span 15 to 18 feet on this move without traveling. It is actually a step-and-a-half move, because on the second step he passes or shoots the ball before the forward foot hits the floor. He releases the ball before two steps are completed. In the fifties I taught my players to use the step-and-a-half around the high-low post area. Two of the more gifted players became very proficient at it. Of course, when they used it in a game, they often had traveling called on them. I would tell my players that if the officials called traveling, the best thing was to stop using the move because "You can't beat city hall." When the two players went on to college, each was told by his coach to quit using the move altogether. That illustrates the degree to which the rule was misunderstood. It took a great offensive move away from their abilities. No doubt, these two coaches discouraged the move because of the approximate 50 percent *turnover* rate when a player used it. About half of the time traveling would be called when a player used the step-and-a-half. It is not how much floor a player covers that determines traveling, it is how the feet are used!

PALMING THE BALL

Many good dribblers today dribble behind the back when changing directions or when their defensive man makes an effort to slap the ball away. This is a great offensive move, but more often than not, the player "palms" the ball when bouncing it behind him, a double-dribble violation. The officials seldom call this violation. Admittedly it is a great move performed by a skillful player, but if officials are not going to call palming of the ball on this behind-the-back dribble, the rule should be changed in some way to make the move legal. The skillful dribbler makes this move so fast sometimes it is difficult to determine whether he palmed the ball or not. In this respect it is different from the 1-2 step on the dunk shot, which is obviously a traveling violation. It is possible to make this move without palming the ball, but much easier to do it well by violating the rule. Since it is seldom called, the players are naturally going to do it the easy way. Many players also tend to carry (palm) the ball for two or more steps when they use the "spin" dribble, again without a violation being called.

An obvious traveling violation *not called* is an injustice to the defense. *Incorrect traveling calls* can upset the whole game of an offensive player. It seems to me that the traveling violation is called too often at the high school level when there is *no violation*, and not often enough at the higher levels, especially in the NBA, when there *is a violation*. Should we not have conformity of the rule at all levels in this important rule infraction? Are not the skilled players playing beyond the rules?

CHARGING OR BLOCKING

In recent years, the Rules Committee has attempted to give the defense a better break on the block or charge call by stressing the responsibility of the offense to avoid contact when the defense has a *legal position* in the path of the offensive drive. This is justified. Such emphasis in calling the charge has encouraged coaches to teach the proper legal defensive position and hold it until contact is made. What clouds the issue on a charge or block is "acting" by the players. For years, only the offensive players put on an act when they thought they were fouled. In the last fifteen years or so, the defense has become more active each year with this "acting" business. Is acting bad for basketball? The purist would say *yes*. The realist accepts it. The latter believes that the competitive nature of the athletes and the fine line in judgment calls will always bring out the "ham" in most players. It's part of the game the officials must contend with. The officials who can spot these "acts" and ignore them are the most respected by the players and coaches.

This relatively new dimension of the defense has only placed a greater burden on the officials. They now have to be alert for the defensive players who try to finesse the charge call when not taking a legal position. However, "acting" *should not keep officials from calling the charge when the defense does have a legal position.* Recently, it has become apparent that many officials ignore the offensive charge. This is usually the best thing to do, if the contact occurs away from the ball. But if it occurs when the offensive player has the ball or immediately after he has passed or shot the ball, it should *not be ignored. It is very discouraging for the player who has learned the art of maintaining a legal defensive position* in an effort to stop an aggressive dribbler. If not called, it also makes it more difficult for a coach to convince his players that it is worth the effort to learn the proper positions in playing good defense. *Besides, offensive players should learn to play under control when dribbling the ball.*

On the other hand, there are many defensive players taking advantage of this emphasis on the rights of the defensive player in maintaining his legal position. This is especially true around the basket. Very often, a player will attempt to draw a foul after the actual play has been completed by positioning himself directly under the basket or beyond (weak side or behind the backboard). Even if the defensive player is stationary before the offensive player leaves his feet for the shot, it is still an attempt to draw a foul rather than stop the shot or player. If the defensive player is unable to get in *front of the basket,* he has been beaten by the offensive player. Defensive players have frequently employed this "trick" successfully for the past few years. I have seen defensive players get this charge call in their favor, even when they were positioned almost out-of-bounds. It is a one-and-one foul call. If he makes both fouls, it nullifies the two points the offensive player earned on the lay-up. The rules should *emphasize* that the defensive man should *be in front of the basket,* in a stationary position, before the offensive player leaves his feet. Being in front of the basket should not be difficult to ascertain.

The game would also be improved if, when a defensive player attempts to draw a foul by taking a charge *away from* the ball (usually weak side) a foul would be called on the defense for attempting to draw this foul.

Allowing a score by an offensive player called for a charge near the basket has always bothered me. When he releases the ball *before* charging into the defensive man, it should *not count.* To be permitted to score when charging only encourages the offensive player to willfully do so. Besides, the official has enough to do in determining whether it is a charge or block, let alone determining if the ball was released before contact was made. This rule tells the offensive players they can score, even if they make illegal moves against the defense. There is no logic to this rule.

SCREENING

Some offenses use illegal screens in movements to free a player for the easy unguarded shot. The term used for this move is "head hunting." Not all so-called head hunting screens are illegal, but many of them are. It is not necessary to go into all aspects of a legal screen, but the same rules apply in what constitutes the legal offensive position in a charge call against the defense. The screener must not be in motion when the contact takes place. He must not slow the defensive player with his arms, legs or hips. Also, a player who sets up a screen *behind* a stationary opponent must not take up a position closer than a normal step from him. The proper way to teach the screen is to have the screener stand in a set position, feet spread to shoulder width. The player using the screen sets up his move with a fake or change of direction, permitting him to cut by the screener. The "head-hunting" screen, where the screener moves into the path of the defensive player in order to screen the player away from an offensive teammate, is illegal. This is the illegal screen that takes place so often in the modern motion or passing man-to-man offense. The rapidity of the screens, plus the close quarters, makes physical contact inevitable while the screener is still moving. Many players make their move to use the screen before the screener is in a set position, which results in an illegal screen. The game would be helped if the officials were more active in calling this illegal screen. The offense would be discouraged from using it. Basketball should be a game of finesse; the illegal screen can make it a game of brute strength and roughness. *The player using the screen should make the screen successful, not the screener.*

DEFENSIVE GOAL TENDING

One of the worst things that can happen to a team, and especially to the player responsible, is to lose a game on a great defensive play. There are so many players now who can block a shot at one to three feet above the basket that the defensive goal tending violation is almost impossible to call with any degree of accuracy under the present rule. The rule states that the block is legal if contact with the ball is made outside the cylinder of the basket and blocked on its way up, and if it has not yet made contact with the backboard. There are several things about this rule that are not good. First, the penalty is too severe. Recently, at a game I was watching a player make a great defensive play near the end of a game. Goal tending was called. Almost everybody close to the play felt the player had made a legal block. This is a difficult call for the official. Players now make legal blocks that are hard to believe. The size and improved jumping of players, especially in the pros and college, reduce this call to guesswork many times. To lose two points on a guess is frustrating, to say the least, and even more so in the closing minutes of the game. When a great defensive play ends by costing points (it happens quite often in games all over the nation), it is time to make the penalty less severe or find a better rule. One part of the rule that should be changed is the one in which goal tending is called on a block after the ball hits the backboard, even though the ball is still definitely on its way up. Many times it is impossible to determine whether the player made contact before it hit the backboard or after. It would be better to call it a legal block, if the ball is going up, no matter when the player makes contact with the ball, whether before or after the ball hits the backboard. There is another thought on this difficult call. Many players now go so high on shots close to the basket that the ball is on its downward flight as it leaves the shooter's hands. It might be better to make the block legal when the defensive player makes contact with the ball outside the cylinder and within three feet (approximate) of the released shot. It would be easier to call than the present rule. It would be a fairer rule for the defense. It would also discourage players from moving to a position near the basket in an attempt to block the shot. They would now be forced to go to the ball in attempting to block the shot, and not to the basket. It is difficult to decide if the suggestions on this rule would help get more consistency on this call. However, under the present rule, the officials are being forced into too much guesswork in making this call.

There are three other rules, which, if changed, could possibly help the game and the officials.

FIVE PERSONAL FOULS

That a player can get into foul trouble easily adds an extra burden on the conscientious official. He does not like to feel responsible for eliminating a player, especially a *top player,* during an important game. This fear tends to subconsciously affect the consistency of his calls during the course of the whole game. Time after time, through the years, I have seen an important player for a team get three personal fouls early in the game, forcing him to the bench for the rest of the first half. An early second-half foul on the player found him sitting again. Maybe three of the four fouls resulted from accidental contact or a questionable call by an official. It is ironic that basketball, a game where "foul trouble" comes easy, is the only game from which a player can be ejected for reasons other than unsportsmanlike conduct. This not only adversely affects the players, but it also subconsciously affects the efficiency of the officials.

Is the elimination of a player after his fifth personal foul necessary? Would it not be better for all concerned—officials, players and coaches—if this outdated rule were changed? Why not, after the fifth foul, allow the coach the perogative of keeping his player in the game or taking him out? If he wishes to leave him in, every foul thereafter on the player in question would give the opponents the ball out-of-bounds on the side in the front court, after the foul shots were made or missed. If it is a common foul, which could be possible, at least in the second half, add a *one shot penalty* and whether made or missed, take the ball again, out-of-bounds on the side.

Certainly this rule change would not increase the number of fouls called in the game or encourage teams to be rougher in their play. Besides, if the player who had accrued the five fouls would begin to get too rough, the official would always be able to put him out of the game for unsportsmanlike conduct. A change in the foul rule similar to the above suggestion would make this phase of the game less burdensome for the officials. The coach could now determine whether a player will play after the fifth violation. The opponents' keeping the ball after shooting the foul is a severe enough penalty that only certain players would be kept in the game after a fifth foul. *Now top players* would not be eliminated in an important game by accidental or questionable fouls. Let's face it, the nature of the rules and the game lets this happen too frequently.

COUNTING BY THE OFFICIALS

Is it possible to eliminate some of the counting the officials have to do in the back court, midcourt and forecourt? Counting accurately while trying to keep up with the action is an impossible task. One of the best arguments for the "thirty second" clock is that it would do away with much of the counting while the ball is "live." The thinking of many who are close to the game is that using a 30-second clock up until the last two minutes of the first and second half would be an improvement. The five second rule in the midcourt and forecourt would be eliminated completely. The less counting the officials had to do, the more they could focus attention on the total action in the game. This freedom from counting would help the officials in overall officiating.

ONE-AND-ONE, OR TWO?

There are three minutes to go and the team in blue is down *five* points. The red team is using the four-corner offense in an attempt to run out the clock. The blue team must get the ball to get back in the game. The strategy of the blue is to play aggressive defense and foul if necessary to get back on the offense. This strategy is obvious to everyone watching the game. A foul is committed by a blue defensive player going for the ball too aggressively and his body makes contact with the offensive player. Was it flagrant or not? This is often very difficult to determine. I have seen what I thought was the obvious flagrant foul draw the "one-and-one" call. This happens too often. In the exciting last minutes of a close basketball game, this type of rule adds unnecessary pressure to the official's duties.

Officials, without a doubt, are struggling with this call. It might be better for the game if all fouls in the last two or three minutes were two-shot fouls for both teams. Most coaches would agree that a team that fouls near the end of a game when leading deserves to pay a two-shot penalty. This would at least make one less judgment call the officials would have to make in the final minutes of a close game. My observation in the last few years has convinced me that the present rule cannot be consistently called with a high degree of accuracy. There must be a better rule to handle these last few hectic minutes for the good of the officials, players, coaches, spectators, and the game itself. (NOTE: A 1983–84 rule change has both teams now shooting two fouls in the last two minutes.)

CONCLUSION

Most officials and coaches with whom all of this has been discussed agree, at least in part, on what is written about the rules in this chapter. I have conscientiously tried to state my convictions that if certain rules in this great game of basketball were modified or changed, it could make the game fairer for participants and less difficult for the officials to call. Basketball, the American game, has been played for almost a hundred years. The game has changed considerably since its inception. *The rules must keep up with this change.* My suggestions are merely an attempt to show the areas in which some changes might accomplish this. After being a part of the game as a player, coach, and official for over fifty years, I will be more content in my retirement for stating these views.

INDEX

257

257

DATE DUE
